Penguin Critical Studies

Richard III

Dr Moseley was educated at Queens' College, Cambridge. He teaches Medieval and Renaissance literature in the University of Cambridge, and in the remissions of this activity confides his thoughts to his word processor which has the double virtue of not answering back and garbling them only on occasion.

For Penguin he has written major studies of Chaucer's *Knight's* and *Pardoner's Tales*, a detailed study of Shakespeare's later *History Plays* (*Richard II*; *1 and 2 Henry IV*; *Henry V: The Making of a King*) and is engaged on an edition of Milton's *Poems published in 1645*. He has also edited and translated for Penguin Classics *The Travels of Sir John Mandeville*, an author for whom he retains his early enthusiasm and whom he feels to be too little known and enjoyed. He is also the author of *A Century of Emblems*, published by Scolar Press.

Penguin Critical Studies
Joint Advisory Editors:
Stephen Coote and Brian Loughrey

William Shakespeare

Richard III

C. W. R. D. Moseley

Penguin Books

PENGUIN BOOKS

Published by the Penguin Group
27 Wrights Lane, London W8 5TZ, England
Viking Penguin Inc., 40 West 23rd Street, New York, New York 10010, USA
Penguin Books Australia Ltd, Ringwood, Victoria, Australia
Penguin Books Canada Ltd, 2801 John Street, Markham, Ontario, Canada L3R 1B4
Penguin Books (NZ) Ltd, 182–190 Wairau Road, Auckland 10, New Zealand

Penguin Books Ltd, Registered Offices: Harmondsworth, Middlesex, England

First published 1989

Made and printed in Great Britain by
Richard Clay Ltd, Bungay, Suffolk
Filmset in Monophoto Times

'There be three degrees of this Hiding and Vailing of a Man's Selfe. The first, Closenesse, Reservation, and Secrecy; when a Man leaveth himself without Observation, or without Hold to be taken, what he is. The second, Dissimulation, in the Negative; when a man lets fall Signes and Arguments that he is not what he is. And the third, Simulation, in the Affirmative; when a Man industriously and expressely faigns and pretends to be that he is not.'

Francis Bacon, 'Of Simulation and Dissimulation', *Essayes or Counsells, civill and morall* (3rd edition, 1625)

Contents

Acknowledgements   viii
Foreword   1

1. Elizabethan Attitudes   5

2. The Theatre and its Role   14

3. History and Political Tragedy   25

4. The Use of the Sources   32

5. The Figure of Richard   43

6. Richard's Performance   58

7. Conscience and the King – Some Themes of the Play   79

8. The Structure of the Play   95

9. Language, Style and Rhetoric   101

Afterword   110

Appendices
    The Text of the Play   113
    Richard's Soliloquies from *3 Henry VI*   115

Further Reading   119

Acknowledgements

Those who encourage others to write books are an often unsung breed of benefactors, for the euphoria of completion often obscures those travails of inception when friends matter. At the beginning the author is grateful for any expressions of confidence that come his way, for he has little himself; in the dark period when the book is half finished and seems to have run into a cul-de-sac a friend's eagerness, however simulated, to see the finished manuscript may stimulate fresh thought, or even – nearly as productive – panic; and when the last touches are being put to the complete thing, perceptive comments and helpful suggestions punctuate even if they do not relieve the tedium of tinkering. All these I have enjoyed from Dr Stephen Coote; without his support – and his commissioning it – the book would never have been written, and I would never have had the huge enjoyment of trying to say what I felt about a play that has fascinated me for twenty years. To Arthur Sale I owe not only a great general scholastic and literary debt, but also gratitude specifically for the comments he made on an earlier publication of mine on this play, which over the years have forced much rethinking and a greater awareness of the complexity of the issues in it. So while its faults are my own, any virtues this book has must be reflections of theirs.

My wife's forbearance, as ever, has been exemplary. It is not taken for granted even if it is being much called upon.

Quadragesima, 1988   C.W.R.D.M.
Reach, Cambridgeshire

Foreword

One of the last works of Robert Greene, who died in 1592 – some say of plague, others of a surfeit of Rhenish wine and pickled herring – is a thinly fictionalized autobiographical tract, *Greene's Groats-Worth of Witte, bought with a Million of Repentance*. At the end of it (Sig. F1, recto) Greene urges his fellow-playwrights to give up writing plays in favour of more godly exercises. One reason is that the market has been taken over by an 'upstart Crow, beautified with our feathers', who 'supposes he is as well able to bombast out a blanke verse as the best of you; and, beeing an absolute *Johannes fac totum*, is in his owne conceit the onely Shake-scene in a countrey'. There is little doubt that this is a reference to Shakespeare; and from the fact that in the same work Greene also parodies a line from *3 Henry VI*, it is clear that the *Henry VI* plays and their apparently huge popularity must be the cause of his back-handed compliment to Shakespeare's ability.

The precise chronology of the first plays in Shakespeare's career, and how far his hand is responsible for the whole of them, are matters that are obscure and likely to remain so. What can be said is that the *Henry VI* plays not only tapped a ready market for plays about the English past, but that the dramatic language the young author was using was immediately recognized to be of an unusual authority. It is also clear that, although *Richard III* is a single dramatic entity of remarkable self-coherence, it is intimately connected to the *Henry VI* plays, may even have been planned in detail before *3 Henry VI* was finished (see p. 47), and is a necessary completion of not only the historical narrative but also of the dramatic, moral and philosophical concerns of the early trilogy.

Dating the play in late 1591, which is very attractive, makes it the earliest play of Shakespeare's we can be certain is all his. It was an immediate success, and remained so for a quarter of a century. Many people believe that Marlowe did not take Greene's advice, and lifted ideas and lines from the *Henry VI* plays and from *Richard III* in *Edward II*: adequate testimony to its immediate recognition as, literally, a masterpiece – a piece of work executed by a young craftsman to show he knew his trade. Not only is it beautifully constructed; it also shows a thorough understanding of how the techniques of the Roman dramatist

1

Seneca, Nero's tutor,* could be adapted to the stage, it shows a command of the resources of language and verse of which a university-educated man would not have been ashamed and it trumps the ace of Thomas Kyd's vastly popular and bloody *The Spanish Tragedy* by being the best horror-play up to that date – without spilling a drop of blood in the theatre. Partly because of this context, when we approach it we may find elements in it crude, artificial, mannered; but we ought to recognize that our judgement of Shakespeare is largely based on the standards he himself set for us in his later, far more experimental, dramas, which broke ground that had not only not been cultivated before but had not even been suspected to exist. If we can approach it without the pre-conceptions of hindsight its excellence will be obvious. It has an intellectual seriousness and consistency, a firmness and economy of structure, and a command of the resources of rhetoric that are in themselves wholly admirable and, in comparison with the work of other dramatists around 1590, quite exceptional.

Getting the play in perspective depends on a number of things. First, it is very easy in an age when most people's only extended acquaintance with Shakespeare is through a printed text to treat it as we would the much later form of the novel. The novel allows the reader to go at his own pace, to flick backwards and forwards through the pages, to zoom in on a passage that catches the attention; and everything that is needed for understanding and evaluation of that understanding is contained in the black marks on white paper. But even with a novel we need some understanding, however shallow, of the period and context in which it was written, or else what it is talking about can easily escape us. That sort of context is even more important with an old play, for the play is not a text: it is an aural and visual experience taking place in a special building, using several sign systems or languages in addition to words. The way words are spoken; the appearance and dress of the actors; the symbolism of the building; the symbolism of the visual pattern formed momentarily on stage; the allusions by words, expression, gesture or pattern to other known and shared ideas – all these have to be taken into account. And, unlike the novel reader, the audience is at the mercy of the director's choice of pace, the actors' emphasis on their lines, the play-wright's order of scenes. There is no chance of stopping the action to ask the company to go back over that bit again. If it is not grasped first time

---

* It should be remembered that originally Seneca designed his plays for recitation and reading rather than production; they are non-naturalistic to a degree, and are *tours de force* of the high art of rhetoric – that is, of using words in elaborate patterns and structures to achieve maximum effect on the reader or audience. See below, pp. 23, 101 ff.

round, it is gone for good. At the lowest level, any successful play of this period has to be dolt-proof. Elizabethan audiences were notoriously unruly, noisy, easily distracted in the press of closely packed humanity in the theatres – as many as 3,000, if we are to believe the accounts of some foreign travellers – and always ready to throw at the actors who did not dominate them the fruit a thoughtful – or cynical – management, always after the maximization of profit, was very prepared to sell them.

All this is obvious enough. In the following pages as a preliminary to discussing the play I shall therefore sketch in its dramatic context and some of the assumptions about the nature of the world on which it relies. I shall also say something of the special cases of history and history plays (particularly as they relate to political commentary) of ideas of tragedy and of the dramatic inheritance. There will be those who feel no need to be told what they know already, and those so fortunate can go straight to p. 25 where my discussion of the play in detail begins.* The strategy of that discussion is to accept the extraordinary dominance of the figure of Richard and use it as a way into the issues of the play. Thus discussion of the structure, form and language comes as a natural conclusion rather than as a preliminary to my analysis.

* There is a much fuller analysis of these issues in general terms in my *Shakespeare's History Plays: 'Richard II' to 'Henry V'* (Penguin, 1988).

1. Elizabethan Attitudes

1. History and Politics

Richard III is only one of a very large number of plays about (mainly English) history from the last two decades of the sixteenth century. (Shakespeare himself wrote nine before 1600 – virtually a quarter of the whole canon of thirty-seven plays, and several of the others have subjects drawn from British or Roman history.) The Elizabethans were intensely interested in their past, seeking in it guidelines for a future that seemed fraught with danger. The old Queen was without a clear heir, and refused to arrange the succession. There had been throughout her reign constant unrest at home and abroad. Although she managed to keep the loyalty of the majority of her Catholic subjects – after all, the admiral who defeated the Armada in 1588 was a Catholic – the religious question was bubbling away like a pressure cooker, and it seemed it could at any time (especially after Pope Pius V in 1570 encouraged good Catholics to conspire against and assassinate Elizabeth) tear the commonwealth of England apart. One had only to glance across to France and the Low Countries to see the terrible havoc caused by religious strife between Catholic and Protestant, and there was no guarantee it could not happen in England. Civil war, dynastic or religious, was a real possibility when the old Queen died, and of course eventually it did come – though not for the expected reasons. The Elizabethans had a perfectly reasonable fear of this most terrible of conflicts, their recent history provided nearly a century of piratical nobles wrangling over the crown, and the wrong done to 'this noble realm of England' is the text to which nearly all the chronicle or history plays of the period are glosses. The revulsion is well expressed in the orotund opening sentence of Hall's *Union of the Noble and Illustre Families of Lancastre and York* (1548), one of Shakespeare's sources for *Richard III*:

What mischief hath insurged in realms by intestine division, what depopulation hath ensued in countries by civil dissension, what detestable murther hath been committed in cities by separate factions, and what calamity hath ensued in famous regions by domestic discord and unnatural controversy, Rome hath felt, Italy can testify, France can bear witness, Beaume [Bohemia] can tell, Scotland can write, Denmark can show, and especially this noble realm of England can apparently declare and make demonstration.

The social and political importance of history is easily forgotten nowadays, when the subject seems for most generally to have been reduced from the high philosophic search for humane understanding to gossip about grandparents, but George Orwell's *1984* contains in a deliberately perverted way an idea which every generation until our own would have understood: 'Who controls the past controls the present; who controls the present controls the future.' The seriousness with which totalitarian regimes, be they fictional or as regrettably real as Hitler's Germany or Soviet Russia, take the past is ample evidence of its importance in forming social and moral values and acting as a yardstick for the present. The Elizabethans, therefore, were not merely curious, or wanting a nice romp through the glamorous exploits of their more successful heroes; they were seeking to understand and evaluate the present, and the history play reached more people more often than any other form of historical discussion. The phenomenon of these plays' existence is a historical and cultural fact of major consequence.

I have indicated that history was a serious and philosophical matter. No attempt to understand the nature and morality of human societies can avoid assuming some theory of the nature of man and the world he lives in. The Greeks and Romans saw history as a series of cycles, where ultimately all returned to its beginning and started again; the Jews and later the Christians introduced the idea that history was a linear process, in which God Himself intervenes, which would one day come to an emphatic end when the meaning of all would be made plain, as the last paragraph of a novel fits the last piece of stone into the arch. (The Marxists have happily taken over the idea of history as a process to a goal, but have ditched the spiritual and theological aspects that give that goal infinitely extensible meaning.) It is, of course, the Christian understanding of human life on earth we have to assume for the reading of Renaissance literature of any kind, and the model of the universe that had developed over many centuries, which accounted for all the known scientific facts at that time, is heavily influenced by Christian thought.

This point is of great importance, for it is astonishing how many people attempt to understand the literature, art and politics of the Renaissance – or any other period – with only the sketchiest and often inaccurate knowledge of a) what Christians believe and b) the Bible. The Bible is, with the remains of Classical literature, the very basis of Western culture and values, constantly fertilizing the minds of succeeding generations, providing values and ideas that really do affect men's behaviour. Any student expecting to be taken seriously, therefore, should get themselves a Bible and read it. We also do our fathers great disservice if we do not bother to find out what understanding of the nature of Man in Christianity it was for which and by which they lived and died – and killed.

2. The Model of the World

The world model is basically to be summed up in the word 'Degree' – that is, an order or rank in which everything in the universe, from the highest seraph to the lowliest element had a specific place, a specific job which only it could do for the glory of God. Virtue, basically, consisted in doing that job, working with the grain of the universe, singing in harmony with it. The idea, current for several centuries and still leaving fossils in our language and thought, is most powerfully expressed in I.iii of *Troilus and Cressida*:

> The heavens themselves, the planets, and this centre,
> Observe degree, priority, and place,
> Insisture, course, proportion, season, form,
> Office, and custom, in all line of order.
> And therefore is the glorious planet Sol
> In noble eminence enthroned and sphered
> Amidst the other; whose med'cinable eye
> Corrects the ill aspects of planets evil,
> And posts like the commandment of a king,
> Sans check, to good and bad. But when the planets
> In evil mixture to disorder wander,
> What plagues and what portents, what mutiny,
> What raging of the sea, shaking of earth,
> Commotion in the winds, frights, changes, horrors,
> Divert and crack, rend and deracinate
> The unity and married calm of states
> Quite from their fixture! O, when degree is shaked,
> Which is the ladder to all high designs,
> The enterprise is sick. How could communities,
> Degrees in schools, and brotherhoods in cities,
> Peaceful commerce from dividable shores,
> The primogeniture and due of birth,
> Prerogative of age, crowns, sceptres, laurels,
> But by degree stand in authentic place?
> Take but degree away, untune that string,
> And hark what discord follows! Each thing meets
> In mere oppugnancy. The bounded waters
> Should lift their bosoms higher than the shores,
> And make a sop of all this solid globe;

> Strength should be lord of imbecility,
> And the rude son should strike his father dead;
> Force should be right, or, rather, right and wrong –
> Between whose endless jar justice resides –
> Should lose their names, and so should justice too.
> Then everything includes itself in power,
> Power into will, will into appetite,
> And appetite, an universal wolf,
> So doubly seconded with will and power,
> Must make perforce an universal prey,
> And last eat up himself.

The basic model of the universe this speech assumes is of a spherical earth at the centre of a series of concentric spheres, each one dominated by living beings whose physical manifestation we perceive as the planets. Those planets move in a great and harmonious dance through the heavens, making the mathematical music of the spheres, inaudible to the ears of those clothed in this 'muddy vesture of decay', as Lorenzo tells Jessica in *The Merchant of Venice* V.i. They pour down on the earth the combined power of their 'influence'. The mainspring of the whole universe is love: the love of God that calls it into existence, the love that his creatures return to him and give to each other. The universe is utterly hierarchical, in a ladder of degree that reaches up to the angels who sing around the throne of God Himself. At the bottom is mere physical matter, composed of its four elements, devoid of life and merely existing. Then come those creatures with the power only to grow and reproduce: the plants. Next on the ladder are those creatures that are not just alive, but have senses: the animals. Man combines these two souls, sensible and vegetable, with a third, the rational – the ability to reason and understand, and he is at the summit of the material creation. Above him are spiritual beings, who are defined by rationality, which they share with man, and the intuitive faculty. Those spiritual beings, angels, rise through Nine Orders or ranks to the highest ranks of all, the cherubim and seraphim who are in the presence of God. Within this basic hierarchy, each order of being has a subsidiary order: the oak is King of trees, the lion of beasts, and man himself is ordered into states and polities having at their head a ruler who is in a position analogous to God at the head of the entire creation, and analogous also to the heads of all other orders. (A fruitful source for the expression of all sorts of ideas, from political persuasion to heraldry to the imagery of plays and poems.) The model therefore implies an understanding of the nature of the universe and human life within it where order, the keeping in one's proper station, is fundamental to peace and harmony, as Ulysses in this speech demonstrates: 'untune that string, And hark what discord follows!'

3. Free Will and the Fall

But if this were all the truth, there would be no room for the calamities that overtake earthly existence and for the active evil that men seek and do. When God made the world through His love, He gave His creatures freedom, according to their capabilities, to choose to serve Him, to love Him, or not. Only if a creature has the capability of not loving, of rejecting love, is the devotion and love it does give of any reality. A universe of automata would know no evil; but it would know no good either. Moreover, God gave the universe and everything in it an existence that ran according to certain complex and intricately linked rules – which our forefathers would have called Nature or 'Kind', and we might call physics; the universe is thus inevitably subject to cause and effect. No action, however small, is without consequences that themselves have consequences till the last syllable of recorded time. The freedom of God's creatures necessarily implies that if they freely give back the love He gives them, the universe runs beautifully, but if they do not, the universe goes sour. And God, by His own rules, His own generosity in giving creatures the dignity of agents, cannot just intervene with a cosmic fire-engine to damp down the trouble that rejection of Him on whom everything depends inevitably brings. Cause will have effect; all moral beings – angels, or men – can do is seek to follow His will even if they are fallen, and all God can do is become Man Himself in a rescue operation from *within* the revolted state.

Free Will therefore entailed necessarily the possibility that some creatures would reject the place or role God had planned for them; and that rejection would dislocate the whole system, and go on doing so, to an extent that would reflect the importance and position of the offender. Lucifer, brightest of all the angels, denied his nature or kind, his creaturely relationship to his maker, becoming Satan, forever racked by the pain of his rejection of what still sustained him. He became the Enemy, a thing of shadows and darkness. Yet Satan still had the power to tempt others by false words and false appearance – and as we shall see Shakespeare deliberately gives Richard just such devilish power. And when Adam fell for Satan's wiles in Eden, all the creation given into his charge was affected too, just as what is on the bottom half of a rope ladder is bound to fall if the ladder has failed higher up. Man's fall brought woe into the world, and Adam's sin is passed on to and warps the existence of all his descendants. But the mercy of God still operates in the free world He gave to His creatures; He still loves and sustains even those who curse him, and the lineaments of the original grand design are everywhere to be seen, giving glory to God.

4. Macrocosm and Microcosm

The model, complete with the idea of the Fall, is in origin at least theological and philosophical. But it is also capable of special applications. The alchemists, to whose work in the sixteenth century a good part of the development of modern science is due, relied on it for their theories of the nature of matter; the political thinker relied on it to understand the mechanisms of human states; the physician and surgeon understood the operations of the human body in terms of a proper balance of the four basic bodily fluids, the Humours, and their proper ordering under Reason, the King of the soul. For the shape of the greater world, the macrocosm, was reflected in every detail within it, and man himself was a little world, a microcosm, organized exactly like a political commonwealth or the revolutions of the spheres. Each affects and reflects the other. Thus a Prince in his parliament is like the sun throned among his planets, at the head of the hierarchy of his kingdom – and the symbolism with which Renaissance men customarily expressed and stressed this idea survives even in the shape and ceremonial of our own Parliament today. A body out of order could be diseased; and so, by an easy transference of ideas, could the state.* Rebellion, for example, is customarily described in precisely the medical term, 'coming to or making a head', that would be used of a rash of spots, or a boil, breaking out on the skin. Similarly, if a King – like Lear – abrogated his station

---

* A Prince could fail of his duty; his subjects then had the difficult moral choice of whether to be obedient and put up with his rule, or to attempt to right it by revolt. In Shakespeare's later tetralogy of history plays, from *Richard II* to *Henry V*, Gaunt says that even a bad King may be best left alone:

> But since correction lieth in those hands
> Which made the fault that we cannot correct
> Put we our quarrel to the will of heaven;
> Who, when they see the hours ripe on the earth,
> Will rain hot vengeance on offenders' heads

> (*Richard II*, I.ii.4–8)

The body politic, sick by the action of its head, might well suffer greater disease, for more likely than the taking of Gaunt's advice was that the subjects would rebel.

and responsibilities, that breaking of order would be reflected in the non-human world: the madness of the King is illustrated by and causes the tempests on the heath. But the inertia of the system was such that, like a spinning top momentarily deflected in its smooth revolution, it would try to right itself and purge the disorder. In that righting the human costs to innocent and guilty alike would be huge. So Richard III's usurpation of the throne, which is itself a symptom of a deep disorder stretching back into history, disturbs the movement of the dance to a degree that can only be put right by general catastrophe that affects the whole of his kingdom; and once introduced, as it was originally by the deposition of Richard II that sparked off the entire sequence of what Shakespeare has taught us to call the Wars of the Roses, disorder or sin persists unto the third and fourth generation. Eventually, in the fullness of time, the discord of man's sin will be resolved into the unbroken concord of the young-ey'd cherubim, just as Lear's madness is eased by music. But the disorders of nations and states are not tractable to sackbuts and hautbois. Blood, horror, violence, war are the purgatives that cleanse the body politic – just what we watch in *Richard III*.

5. The Failure of the Model

The imaginative force of the model is due not only to its having survived and developed in an intricacy now hardly imaginable over many centuries – so that the languages spoken throughout Europe today are deeply affected by it – but also to the fact that it accounted for a good deal of the mysteries of human existence. But it did not account for all, and as we all can now know, in certain rather fundamental respects the model was plain wrong. (That is not to say it has not still got a moral or mythic truth we could attend to with profit.) As a physical description of the universe, it was coming under increasing attack in the sixteenth century; as a theory on which to base technological and scientific work, it was challenged, eventually successfully, throughout the seventeenth century; as a way of understanding politics and human behaviour, it was simply not accounting for all the facts – and it never had done, however beautiful the theory. In his later tetralogy, *Richard II, 1 and 2 Henry IV, Henry V*, Shakespeare devotes a great deal of attention to the validity of the model as a diagnosis of the human condition, and the only answers he suggests are equivocal. Later, in *Troilus and Cressida*, the powerful speech of Ulysses I have quoted is in a context ironic in the extreme, for the play is one which examines the breakup of these very ideas in the way men behave as moral and political animals. Shakespeare, man of his time as

11

he was, undoubtedly felt the emotional and moral force of the old ideas that together formed the old model, but he is also aware that men who refuse consent to be bound by this vision of order have, *ipso facto*, a terrible power against those who do. The resourcefulness of evil is unbounded; good by its very nature is vulnerable even if, generations of innocent suffering later, it is ultimately victorious. And what sort of a victory is it that has to be established by the pointless suffering of the innocent? *King Lear* gives us a terrible vision of the universal wolf's career before the balance that alone makes societies workable is in some way restored – but the suffering that precedes and conditions that restoration is so appalling that the memory of it simply cannot be forgotten nor its meaning fully understood.

Richard III does not yet go as deep as this, but even in this early play Shakespeare is interested in the problem. Like Edmund in *King Lear*, King Richard III is just such a universal wolf, as the imagery of beasts of rapine and violence applied to him reminds us; he is the 'new man', the disciple of Machiavelli (see p. 53), who rejects the conventions of civilized human society. But while he devastates his country, the play stresses the irony that in the end he is not only acting as an unwitting agent of Heaven's vengeance on people who are self-evidently and self-confessedly guilty – and for most of whom we feel scant pity – but calling forth by his so acting a response which destroys him. At last he eats up himself. In this play at least, Heaven seems to be acting on the strictest positivist principle of justice, an eye for an eye and a tooth for a tooth. A facile view would be to hold that Richmond's succession means that the universe's order is vindicated after the generations of crime, but to it, even in this highly patterned early play, we could give no more than a hesitant consent. For among all the guilty sufferers, there are the innocent and pathetic figures of the two Princes, and Shakespeare underlines that because the settlement is so dependent on the character of the ruler, only an interim of equilibrium has been reached. There is no assurance that bottled spiders are now extinct for good.

To discern a pattern of human history, particularly against this background of a cosmic and moral theory, is therefore of fundamental importance to men's understanding of the nature of the world they inhabit: an understanding that partly conditions that world. Shakespeare never throughout his career lost interest in the topics of guilt, innocence and consequence:

> The evil that men do lives after them;
> The good is oft interred with their bones

– and at the end of his career, in *The Tempest*, he returns to a discussion of the relationship between real suffering in the past and new growth and fruitfulness in the future.

1. The Theatre and its Role

1. The Seriousness of Drama

The theatre amused and diverted, and if it failed to do that it did not make a living in a very competitive market for the members of the companies. And although by definition what we see on the stage is not 'the real thing', but a representation through illusion, neither that nor its amusement value prevents its being a highly self-conscious and serious intellectual pursuit, recognized as such by audiences and playwrights, actors and critics. The profundity of Shakespeare's concerns and their analysis in his plays may be unusual in degree, but those concerns are by no means untypical of his fellow-dramatists.

The assumptions behind the theatre are every bit as important to us in approaching an old play as are assumptions about the world, and we need briefly to examine some of the conventions that operate both in the idea of drama and in its techniques.*

Fundamentally, drama is a shared group experience and has close links to other public group experiences like religious ritual.† In ancient Greece, indeed, the drama developed within the context of public religious festival, and never lost its connection with it. The great tragedians of the Classical period handled mythical history with the explicit aim of exploring the nature of man, his relation to the gods and the moral and consequential restraints on human life. The historical truth of the story of, say, Oedipus, mattered little when weighed against the issues of guilt, the moral order of the universe, and the effects of suffering that Sophocles' play, for example, explores. The audience's emotional response was fact enough. The decline of town life in late Antiquity and the consequent shrinking of resources available for public drama to all intents and purposes killed it except as a literary entertainment for the solitary. But the need to act out the really deep

---

* The word 'convention' is one we shall meet again. Briefly, it may be defined as an area of silent agreement between author and audience, where the referent need not be stated. Conventions exist on the levels of symbolism, gesture, language, character and plot; and properly used convention is a great help in achieving economy and force of expression.

† It might be as well to remind ourselves of one common derivation of the word religion from 'religare', to bind together: in much Roman thought, religion was the binding together of Gods and men, and religious studies thus becomes the examination of the moral and ethical relationships of individuals and communities to their world.

concerns of human beings seems to be endemic, whether we are looking at the cave painting of Lascaux, the hunting rituals and dance-narratives of the Red Indians or the drama of Greece; and when in the ninth and tenth centuries European society is once again beginning to provide the conditions where men and women can live together in some sort of security, we find a new beginning of drama. Interestingly, it begins again, as it did in Greece, in the context of the most holy areas of experience. The earliest drama we have is very simple: just the division of the reading of the Gospel for Easter Day between several readers. But as soon as the Gospel narrative of the visit of the three Marys to the garden is thus split up, we have dialogue; their experience of finding the empty tomb is re-enacted in the context of a ritual that is itself a re-enactment of Our Lord's words and commands on the night that He was betrayed.

2. Mysteries and Moralities

This extremely primitive play was capable, step by tiny step, of almost infinite extension, into a sequence that dramatized the whole Biblical narrative from creation to Last Judgement. If the Easter Gospel, why not the Annunciation to the Shepherds, or the visit of the Magi – and so on. Soon the drama became too big to remain a mere incident in the Mass in the church building, however great the advantages of the complex symbolism of that building as a setting for it; the next step is literally outside, to the churchyard, where the drama is independent of the liturgy; and thence it goes into the highways and byways. The drama that developed down to the late Middle Ages is almost entirely religious, and the great cycles of plays, produced by the craft guilds or 'mysteries',* were played throughout Europe until well after the Renaissance. These plays have no lack of subtlety, but necessarily they are in the basic outlines of their plot and characterization of main historical personages bound by the Biblical narrative and, as time went by, by the conventions established for their effectiveness by earlier plays. Their seasonal recurrence becomes an important punctuation mark in community life and, behind the slapstick comedy, the grotesquery, the deliberate creation of detailed realistic illusion within the recognizably artificial and unrealistic format of the plays, lie the deadly serious issues of Hell or Heaven for each and every one of the spectators.

The restriction imposed by the Biblical sequential historical narrative

* Latin *ministerium*, 'trade', gives us French *métier* as well as English 'mystery'. Craft secrets and skills were literally mysterious to those who did not know them.

on the main plots of the mystery plays meant that certain issues of real general moral importance could not easily be discussed. Later in the Middle Ages, therefore, there develops a form of drama which uses many of the techniques and presuppositions of the mysteries while cutting itself free from the historical plot: the morality play. These plays employ the techniques of personification and allegory to a very large degree to explore often generalized moral issues; and many of them are dramatizations of 'soul-battles' or psychomachia. The incomparable *Everyman* is an excellent example of the type: the central character is Mankind, and facets of his personality, or the pressures on that personality, are personified in a struggle for his salvation. This form of drama remained popular until late in the sixteenth century, and in its use of symbolic, personified abstract figures for characters, its disregard for naturalism and its central moral interest it is clearly one of the ancestors of the important masque form. It could also be adapted for the discussion of history and politics, as John Skelton's *Magnyfycence* (1530?) or John Bale's *King John* (1534?) make clear. Moreover, the nature of its characters, often very vividly detailed but at the same time symbolic, has general relevance to the Elizabethan drama that grows in part from it: we find that characters who do not at first sight appear to be allegorical may carry a symbolic overtone. For example, the banishment of Kent in the first act of *King Lear* strongly resembles the banishment of Good Counsel by a foolish King in political Moralities, and we are alerted as to how to take and value a figure like Malvolio in *Twelfth Night* by his generalizing name. The handling of Richard III has close links with this sort of characterization (see below, p. 48).

Both these types of play are ultimately comic in vision, and we need to bear this in mind when looking at *Richard III* which, as we shall see, depends heavily on them and on consequent audience expectations. I do not use 'comic' to imply that there was a laugh a minute; rather, to mean that whatever the immediate horror and suffering represented, ultimately the Mercy of God was there for the taking. In the words of the fourteenth-century mystic Lady Julian of Norwich, 'All things shall be well, all manner of thing shall be well.' The Christian perspective of this drama constantly reminded its audience that the sacrifice of Christ had opened the road to heaven for even the most hardened sinner if he would take it; that the power of the devil and all his angels was finally broken. The power of the devil is still frightening and real, and men can still, through succumbing to temptation and not repenting, damn themselves for eternity; but the devil exercises his power on sufferance, his energy is comic in that, devoted to spiting God by harming the trees in His garden, the devil is sawing through the branch on which he sits – and is too stupid in his cleverness to see it. A major feature of the morality drama is the exposing of the devil's activities and temptations for what they are, despite the attractive appearance to human eyes he well knows how to give them: for, as Scripture tells us, the devil can appear in the likeness of an angel of light. Men can still fall into Hell by their own choice, and that may be terrible. But the texture of the world is still ultimately optimistic.*

Both these classes of play are obviously closely connected with preaching. Preaching had as its main aim not only instruction but also making the hearer feel what intellectually he knew – to engage, by story and anecdote, the imagination of the audience in understanding their own moral predicament. Just as Hamlet saw that the play was the thing wherein to catch the conscience of the King, so the medieval and Renaissance dramatists laid snares for the consciences of their spectators to save them from the pains of Hell.

3. Symbolism

The moral seriousness of this earlier, and contemporary, drama is part of Shakespeare's inheritance – it is impossible he did not see these plays – and like other dramatists of the time he draws on many of its symbols and characters quite openly in drama that is not at all religious in any strict sense. (The structure of the plot of *Richard III*, and the characterization of Richard himself, owes much to the techniques of the Moralities: see p. 48ff.) Some of those symbols concern its staging: a pageant cart, for example, might have a superstructure to represent Heaven and its space between the huge wheels might represent Hell: the surface of the cart is thus this world. A temporary scaffold could easily be made more openly symbolic, and when Hamlet jumps around the stage in near hysteric merriment on hearing the ghost in the cellarage of the Globe, it is precisely this symbolism Shakespeare is drawing on. For the Elizabethan theatre's inheritance meant that it was inevitable that the buildings that were devised to accommodate theatrical performance would be symbolic in the symbolic language with which people were already familiar.

---

* *Dr Faustus*, which draws heavily on morality-play themes and techniques, is thus hardly to be seen as a tragedy in any modern sense of the term: it is, in the grim old sense of the term, farcical. Faustus misuses his freedom to choose damnation, and the play marks out step by step the self-ruining of a once great intellect into stupidity and folly. Grace is open to him even at the last, but he rejects it.

From contemporary accounts, stage directions, lists of properties, lines and cues in plays and so on it is clear that, however different they may have been, the dozen or so theatre buildings that were operating in London in the years around 1600 could be used symbolically. Over the stage was spread the 'Heavens', and in one theatre at least this canopy seems to have been painted with representations of the zodiac and heavenly bodies. Through it trapdoors allowed the descent of gods on to the human level of the world, the stage – as 'Juno' does in *The Tempest* or Jupiter in *Cymbeline*. Below was the cellarage where the ghost in *Hamlet* is heard moving. Props too could be as symbolic as anything in the Moralities or mysteries: it is known that the Admiral's Men had a 'Hell Mouth' – in all probability a huge lath and canvas representation of a gaping whale's or dog's mouth, through which sinners could be dragged, as Faustus is.

Thus the theatre conventionally mirrored the world not as it might on the surface appear, but as a moral and spiritual reality lying behind appearance; and even in history plays and comedies we need to keep this possibility in mind.

The force of this special and symbolic building is increased if we reverse its metaphor. In the last decades of the sixteenth century there is growing insistence on the equivalence of 'world' and 'theatre'. If the theatre represents the world, the world is a theatre, where men play parts, consciously or not, in a serious drama on which their salvation depends. The metaphor of 'all the world's a stage' is too well known to need further exploration; but the bitter frisson underlying it is well expressed by one of Walter Ralegh's poems about what he called, in the preface to his *Historie of the World*, 'this stage-play world':

> What is our life? A play of passion;
> Our mirth the music of division;
> Our mothers' wombs the tiring houses be,
> Where we are dressed for this short comedy.
> Heaven the judicious sharp spectator is,
> That sits and marks still who doth act amiss;
> Our graves that hide us from the searching sun
> Are like drawn curtains when the play is done.
> Thus march we playing to our latest rest –
> Only we die in earnest, that's no jest.

The grim ambiguity of the semantics of these lines makes us recognize the seriousness with which the theatre metaphor could be taken; and in *Richard III* there is no character more self-conscious about his role-playing and acting than Richard, or more ironically focused by the knowledge the audience have of what the 'judicious sharp spectator' is doing.

The illusion of the theatre, then, is one that is inseparable from the reality that it imitates and affects. It is in any case in the nature of drama that real experience and emotion is attached to illusory happenings; but that response acquires a new complexity when the happenings are an interpretation not of a fiction but of a datable historical happening – as in this play. The audience's response to the illusion becomes even more crucially part of the play's subject, and Richard's peculiar relationship to an audience that strictly he could not know existed makes audience reaction to the observed events part of the subject of the play and indeed part of its plot. A play where the hero is *par excellence* an actor is *ipso facto* a play about playing.

And, to some extent, about playwriting. For this play, like any other, is not a continuum of events as they occurred in all their untidiness. The plot is an interpretation of events, not even a mere story; a process has gone on of shaping, selection and juxtaposition of happenings. We should never ignore, as we often tend to, the sequence of scenes in a Renaissance play, and particularly how they are juxtaposed. For just as in, for example, news on television the cutting from one shot to the other, or the choice of camera angle can speak worlds of comment without a word being said, so the sequence of scenes is an important part of the interpretation of the events. The very fact that *Richard III* opens with that extraordinary soliloquy, which acts almost like an Induction to a masque, throws an ironic light over everything that happens later. The playwright's control over his material, within the obvious limits in a history play, is total, and he is less interested in recounting events than drawing out their significance.

4. Theories of Drama

For the playwright shares with his audience the expectation that, whatever else it might do, a play could raise serious moral issues, and not to do so would be as significant as doing so. The inheritance from the Morality tradition determines one sort of expectation of drama author and audience would have. But in addition the more educated would be aware of the growing body of theoretical philosophical criticism that took drama seriously. Aristotle's *Poetics* was rediscovered in the late fifteenth century, and has been discussed ever since. The book relates drama to psychology and moral philosophy, and the sixteenth-century commentators on Aristotle are much exercised to account for and elucidate the views of one who had enormous weight as one of the founders of Western philosophy. Francisco Robortello, for example, whose commentary appeared in 1548, sees drama as holding up examples of morality and virtue to be imitated by an audience whose emotional response has engaged them with the characters. J. C. Scaliger, whose work was greatly influential for a century after it appeared in 1561, stresses that the poet has a responsibility for the moral education of his audience,* teaching them how to avoid bad actions in favour of good. Poetry – which includes drama – is for him related to ethics and politics, and assists the community towards achieving harmony or happiness through proper action, assisted by the representation of good models. We can be sure that this discussion – which is more complex than I have indicated – was known in England; Sir Philip Sidney's *Defence of Poesie* (1595) shows a thorough understanding of the terms of the debate, and it is quite clear that Shakespeare knew all about it too. For Sidney and Shakespeare the high art of the poet lies not in mere imitation of things as they are, but in the representation of things as they could or should be – an expression of an ideal which will fire the imagination to acts of virtue.

The application of these ideas to plays dealing with the real events of history is complex. The contemporary understanding of history and historiography, and the nature of the history play – even if it is not described as a 'tragedy', as *Richard III* is (see below pp. 23, 27) – will have considerable bearing on the audience's possible response to a drama, and set some limits to the playwright's freedom in writing it. If, moreover, the play is defined as a tragedy, a literary form which is related to history, further expectations are triggered.

5. History and Tragedy

The concepts of history our fathers held are not the same as ours. For us, history has become in the main the structural study of whole societies: the minutiae of parish records, cotton workers' diet sheets and the unreliable reminiscences of garrulous geriatrics are as important and relevant – to use a vogue word – as any amount of political events. What

---

* Note the huge irony Shakespeare focuses on Richard if we bring this idea into play: Richard, acting a part, stage managing others, even suggesting what is to be said to the Mayor and citizens, is in some sense a playwright in league with the audience. But his motives are far from virtuous, he invites delight in crime and trickery – yet is upstaged by the audience's knowledge of his future and Shakespeare's manipulation of him.

seems to be the aim is the achievement of a feeling of 'what it was like', *how* things have got to the state they have – an understanding (doomed to be partial) of a vastly complex social machine without letting value judgements creep in. In the past – even the quite recent past – history was something else again. Dionysus of Halicarnassus first made the often quoted remark that 'History is Philosophy teaching by examples', and we would do well to remember that for our ancestors philosophy – the pursuit of wisdom – was one of the highest human endeavours. Wisdom is not just knowledge, but understanding of the context and meaning of that knowledge; ultimately it aims at a moral, even a theological or devotional end. There is good Biblical authority for the importance of this quest in the Proverbs and the Wisdom of Solomon, and good pagan authority, to mention only the works of Plato, or Aristotle,* or Epictetus. If history is then subservient to philosophy, as Dionysus' remark implies, it follows that the reading of history will ultimately be a moral activity, an attempt to understand the nature of the human predicament by study of individual examples. The historian's job was not primarily to do with chronology, or even with the mechanisms of society: it was to range across the wide fields of Time, gathering men and events and seeking to understand the principles of human conduct.

English history is, of course, included in the concept of history as a process with a purpose to it I mentioned above (p. 6). It too was therefore a continuum, where modern men were deeply affected by their forefathers and would equally deeply affect their sons. Even for people of slight education, therefore, English history – and the watching of plays about it – could not be other than relevant to their own concerns. Even today most people regard history at its lowest level as providing cautionary examples, and modern politicians often appeal to history – however bogus – to justify their stances to their potential voters. 'Remember 1945' or 'Remember Munich' are simply updated versions of remembering Henry V or Richard III. The topical issues in Shakespeare's day could only be discussed by appeal to the evidence they had, that from history. A playwright who tackles the difficult ideas of political legitimacy, of the nature of kingship, of the relationship between Prince

---

* Aristotle's remark in the *Poetics* that tragedy is more philosophical than history is rather important in the context of this book: both are concerned with the pursuit of wisdom, but because tragedy, which is based on happenings (or what might believably happen), escapes the demands for factual accuracy that limit history, it is freer to search for significance and meaning and express those things through its form and shape. Aristotle is also suggesting that tragedy teaches wisdom in its own right, and is thus closely related to the highest discipline, philosophy.

and country – all very much discussed in the unhappy years at the end of the sixteenth century – is going to find himself drawn inescapably to history. The history of England that Shakespeare uses in his plays allows author and audience to come to terms with themselves, to work out their values in a communal and serious activity, to formulate, express, evaluate their ideals. The playwright, then as now, both responds to and modifies preoccupations and issues in society and formulates them (it is arguable which comes first). A society much concerned about legitimacy of succession, succession itself, and the nature of the ruler's title – ultimately about fallen man's position *vis-à-vis* God – must discuss these issues. In its understanding of the past – or at least isolation of its problems – it may well find the means to discuss those contemporary problems which, because they were too intimate, too important to be easily handled openly, could not be approached by any other means.

Let us now glance at the notion of tragedy and the expectations the word carried for a Renaissance audience. In late medieval tradition, tragedy simply meant, as Chaucer makes his Monk put it,

> Tragedie is to seyn a certeyn storie,
> As old bokes maken us memorie,
> Of him that stood in greet prosperitee
> And is yfallen out of heigh degree
> Into miserie, and endeth wrecchedly.
>
> (*Canterbury Tales*, VII, 1973–7, B83163–7)

There is no question here of any particular moral type of person – in fact the Monk's tales include people whom we would not call even in a loose sense tragic; it is the fall that matters, and the fall of the great exemplifies the great power of Fortune in human affairs. Tragedy, as a genre, is thus both historical and cautionary; the chief lesson to be learnt is the instability of the world. It is to a great extent this sort of tragedy, and this sort of expectation of it, that makes up the narrative collection of the *Mirror for Magistrates* (see below, p. 40), an important source for *Richard III*. Even when Shakespeare develops the idea of tragedy further than it ever had been taken before, in *King Lear*, he never entirely abandons this link with Fortune; his insight is to connect the operation of Fortune with the moral activity of men.

But other ideas of tragedy were current and new ones were being introduced and explored. The tragedies of Seneca, the Roman poet and Stoic philosopher who, once tutor to Nero, was forced by that ungrateful emperor to commit Stoic suicide, were well known to men of education. At a time when Greek drama was hardly known at all, all his nine extant plays on stories from Greek mythology were translated between 1559 and 1581, and they were much admired and their methods imitated. Seneca designed his plays for reading and for recitation, to inculcate the ideals of Stoic philosophy – the pursuit of virtue, resignation in the face of catastrophe, a disregard for most of the things men commonly seek, like health, wealth, success or pleasure, so that reason could be followed undisturbed by the lower emotions of pain, pleasure, desire or fear. The stories of Hercules or Medea were admirable vehicles for this; and there is much in Stoic philosophy that is attractive to a Christian society. Moreover, the authority of Seneca as a major writer of Antiquity (who until the later Middle Ages was believed to have corresponded with St Paul and even to have become a Christian) led not only to the taking seriously of what he had to say but to the imitation of his method of saying it. In his plays he gives his characters a high, even exaggerated, style; their declamatory speeches are rhetorically complex, their dialogue frequently falls into the rapid exchange of balanced, patterned lines known as stichomythia, and their action is framed by a Chorus that observes, comments on and provides a context for the action. The plays are full of narrated horror, bloodthirsty details, ghosts, magic. It will be immediately obvious that there is a good deal of Senecan influence in the writing and indeed the structuring of *Richard III*, and I shall examine that later; but for the moment the important thing is that the Senecan tradition in sixteenth-century drama redoubles the insistence on it as moral and philosophical instruction.* Furthermore, the renewed interest which I have already mentioned in Aristotle's analysis of Greek tragedy in the *Poetics* has given rise to a good deal of serious consideration of the term – and, indeed, of the theory of drama as a whole. Aristotle emphasized that if tragedy was to achieve in the audience what he saw as the desirable effect of the purifying of the emotions of pity and fear (i.e. their redirection from trivialities to the serious issues of the human condition, and a sense of the dignity of man), certain things were necessary; the hero must be important, but he must also be recognizably a man like ourselves, who is neither impossibly good nor impossibly bad; his fall must spring from some flaw in his character, and must be the result of a chain of events that do not merely follow each other but are causally linked. His fall must also be just, however terrible it may be. Here there is a clear emphasis on the moral nature of tragedy; it is moral in the motivation

---

* It is worth recalling that in Cap. III of one of the favourite reference books of the Renaissance, Natalis Comes' *Mythologiae siue Explicationum fabularum libri decem* (Venice, 1568), tragedy is classed as a political *fable* – that is, the story has a concealed moral meaning more important than the surface narrative.

of the plot, moral in the examination of the problem of the justice of events and moral in the effects on the audience. Tragedy is thus a means of interpreting our human predicament, not merely of contemplating the instability of Fortune.

When *Richard III* is called a tragedy, then, we have to take all these views into account. It delineates the rise and deserved fall of Richard and shows how even when he thinks he is most in control Fortune can tip the scale against him; it is certainly cautionary, and may be even more topically so that we easily realize (see below, p. 25f); the course of the play is deeply concerned with the notion of justice and the role of Providence in human affairs. But the play does not have that sense of the dignity of humankind and sense of appalling waste we experience in watching Lear, Macbeth, Hamlet, or Othello as, partly through their own fatal error, the machinery of the universe grinds them exceeding small. In Richard III's case the laugh is on him from the very beginning; the audience may enjoy his amoral energy, but knows that he will get his deserved and expected comeuppance at Bosworth.

By signalling to the audience that the play is a tragedy (and using the appropriate form for one – see p. 98f), at the very least Shakespeare is telling them to contemplate the vicissitudes of human life; by taking his material from well-known and topical English history, he is removing the subtle barrier between what can be conveniently categorized as 'story' and what is painful in the here and now – exactly as today a play (like Hochhuth's *Soldiers*) or television programmes about the recent past, or about heroic figures who are only recently dead, like Winston Churchill, make the shoe pinch. This exploitation of historical event represents a challenge to thought and involvement, and rules out the indifferent response. Richard III really mattered in English history, and no Elizabethan could not have a view about him. Just as Greek tragedians took their plots from mythical history that everyone knew and accepted as in some way paradigmatic of the puzzle of existence, so Shakespeare takes his from the history he could count on his audience knowing, and turns their attention to the examination of the very nature of the world – political, ethical, moral, cosmic – they take so readily for granted.

Richard III, history play and tragedy (in however limited a sense) as it is, therefore defines itself as both morally serious and highly relevant to contemporary issues in general terms. But it is more than that; it is topical to a degree.

3. History and Political Tragedy

That history plays were expected to be relevant to contemporary political and moral concerns is abundantly clear. What may surprise us – though it should not, perhaps – is the way they could be used as disguised comment on the pressing issues of the moment.* *Richard III* is no exception; well before Shakespeare wrote the play, the figure of the hunchback King is extensively used both to illustrate the idea of political Machiavellianism (see below and pp. 54ff) as an idea and to comment on particular statesmen.

An anonymous tract, the *Treatise of Treasons*, appeared in 1572, when nervousness about Catholic plots against Elizabeth was intense. It was written from a pro-Catholic standpoint, and had two main aims: to defend the Catholic Duke of Norfolk and Mary Queen of Scots against the charges of sedition that were being bandied about, and to prove that treason was to be feared from another quarter: from the activities of the Queen's ministers, William Cecil and Sir Nicholas Bacon, all the more dangerous as they were trusted. The writer makes his targets the 'Machiavels' and 'Catilines'† who are seeking to destroy the basis of an ordered society. The Machiavellian libertines,‡ he says, have destroyed as a matter of policy the old religion, leaving the common folk with nothing to put in its place: ... a 'Machiavellian State and Regiment: where Religion is put behind in the second and last place: where the civil Policie, I meane, is preferred before it, and not limited by any rules of Religion, but the Religion framed to serve the time and policy ...' (A travesty – if an understandable one – of the Elizabethan understanding of the relationship between Prince and Church.) He makes a specific parallel between the hidden plots of the

* A fuller treatment of the issue will be found in my *Shakespeare's History Plays*.
† Catiline was organizer of a very dangerous conspiracy against the constitutional government of the Roman Republic in BC 63; he was outwitted and defeated by Cicero. Cicero wrote a notable speech against him, and the historian Sallust's account of the affair was much read in the Renaissance. Catiline was a man of real ability and charm, who was able to blind his many supporters to his true nature and purposes. Ben Jonson's tragedy, *Catiline* (1611), indicates something of the contemporary interest in this figure and the type of politician he epitomized.
‡ The choice of the word – a neat smear – implies that his targets have made their own desires and will the arbiters of their actions – a highly immoral position.

time and the devious actions of Richard III in seeking the crown. It is therefore clear that by 1572 at least Richard must have been an acceptable and accepted archetype of Machiavellianism, and that smearing comparison to him could be damaging.

Later, many pamphlets were directed against the ascendancy of Elizabeth's favourite, Robert Dudley, Earl of Leicester. His father, the Duke of Northumberland, had played a very important part in the events during and just after the reign of Edward VI, and quite clearly had attempted, by arranging the marriages of his children, to secure the throne for his descendants and permanent political power for himself. Mary's accession had ruined him, but he nearly succeeded; and some of the suspicion the father had justified transferred itself to the son. Leicester was undoubtedly ambitious, was connected to and patron of the house of Huntingdon, in whose veins ran the last Plantagenet blood in England – they descended from George, Duke of Clarence – and almost certainly had hopes of marrying Elizabeth before the suspicious death (by poison, it was rumoured) of his secret wife, Amy Robsart, so ruined his reputation as to put paid to any such scheme. (Whether Elizabeth, consummate politician that she was, ever had any such designs is much more debatable: had she done so, at a stroke she would have alienated half the peerage of England, on whose support her insecure throne depended.) Yet the Queen recognized Leicester's ability and had the good sense to keep him with her – which did not please influential factions in the state. One of the most famous of the libels against him is *A Copie of a Leter, wryten by a Master of Arte of Cambridge* (sometimes called *Leicester's Commonwealth*) which appeared in English in 1584 and then, with a much more inflammatory title, in French. Leicester, a 'Machiaveliste' (as the French title calls him) is accused of all sorts of murders and crimes, and frequently Richard III's crimes and ambitions are likened to Leicester's. He is accused of seeking for his own advantage to divert the crown away from the true heirs, the house of Scotland, to the house of Huntingdon – which he is deceiving, for 'he will not be so improvident, as to make him his soveraign, who now is but his dependent'. (The comparison to Buckingham and Richard III is apt.) He is accused of unbounded jealousy and ambition in trying to marry Elizabeth and in trying to marry his son to another claimant to the throne, Arabella Stuart. A damaging comparison is made between the Amy Robsart affair and Richard III seeking to marry Elizabeth of York while Anne Neville was, reputedly, still alive. Many of his stratagems are attributed to Machiavelli. Even Sir Philip Sidney's impassioned defence of his uncle did not prevent some of the mud sticking.*

The detailed comparisons, of which these few examples will suffice, between Richard III and members of Elizabeth's Council, make it quite clear that his career and character were seen as paradigmatic long before Shakespeare wrote his play. He is used as a mirror of usurpation and tyranny – political concerns that are at the very centre of English politics in the sixteenth and seventeenth centuries – and as an example *par excellence* of the political Machiavellian. His defeat by Richmond, which put a stop to nearly a century of kinstrife, can thus be seen as a victory of Good over devilish Evil, and something earnestly to be admired: for renewal of the horrors of civil war was feared with very good reason by the Elizabethans (but see below, pp. 89–90). Shakespeare's play, therefore, cannot but be topical to an audience that as a general rule had the current relevance of history constantly in mind; and it may be even more politically sensitive than we realize. Shakespeare, and the Lord Chamberlain's Men, the company of which he was by 1591 a member, do not seem to have been afraid to get involved in political issues. The relationship between them and Elizabeth's last favourite, Robert Devereux, Earl of Essex later in the decade suggests that for one reason or another they took sides then against the continuing power of the Cecils and, given the tension in England after the defeat of the Armada in 1588, it is impossible not to wonder how *Richard III* would have sounded.

Richard III is called a tragedy in the Quartos; and the Folio editors retained this classification while nevertheless putting it in with the group of histories. It would be foolish to claim that these labels of history and tragedy imply rigid division of genre and therefore of expectations and areas of interest – indeed, this play as well as the Ricardian tetralogy clearly indicates that Shakespeare had no such clear distinction in his mind; nevertheless, they are not meaningless terms, as we have seen, and do imply different areas of emphasis.

Renaissance moral thought, in poets as well as philosophers, recognized a distinction between the ethical issues that affected a private person and

---

* The writer of this attractive work may well have been the Jesuit Robert Parsons. He wrote several works attacking Elizabeth and her ministers, and argued strongly against the legitimacy of her rule and the morality of the Church/State relationship she had set up. English Catholics, who had a difficult enough row to hoe, may well have felt that with a friend like him enemies were unnecessary. It was probably he who in 1592, four years after Leicester's death, circulated *A Declaration of the True Causes of the great troubles, presupposed to be intended against the realme of England*, in which all these charges are renewed against old Cecil. But here the references to Richard III are absent.

the political morality that governed his public life. Spenser's letter to Ralegh that prefaces the incomplete *Faerie Queene* illustrates just this: the twelve private virtues will be discussed in the person of Prince Arthur and, after he has become King, the twelve politic virtues. Now the discussion of tragedy by Aristotle and his commentators, as well as the evidence of existing Renaissance plays, suggests that while the subjects of tragic drama may well be persons of great political and public importance, the focus of interest is firstly on what the course of events does to them as people and, secondly, on how we respond to their suffering. Thus tragedy could be said to deal primarily with the moral world of the individual at the centre of events. History and history- or chronicle-plays, on the other hand, necessarily see the individual (who may well be proper material for tragedy) as contributing to a large-scale sequence of events where the interest is primarily in the meaning of the historical process. The distinction can be illustrated, perhaps, by a quick glance at *Richard II* and the *Henry IV* plays. In the former, we are deeply interested in the nature of Richard as he relates to his role as King, in the growth of his understanding of that role – particularly when he can no longer discharge it – and in his understanding of his personal responsibility for the chaos into which his rule has fallen. He is genuinely tragic in both the medieval and Aristotelian senses (see above, p. 22f). But Richard's tragedy is a major element in a historical process that extends over a huge span of time, long after Richard's death. Its meaning cannot be seen within any one lifetime. And so the *Henry IV* plays, while not denying potentially tragic status to Henry IV, are carefully designed to make us repeatedly see the events against a backdrop of extended time and the characters as ironized by what we know and they cannot. One of Shakespeare's most brilliant strokes is to use an image-cluster constantly recurring through the two plays so that the real reference point of individual action becomes a nebulous but powerful figure of personified England, bleeding with the wounds of her children. As a result, we are much more interested in the issue of, 'What is this doing to England?' than, 'What is it doing to X?'

Richard III seems to be a hybrid of these two types of play. It is certainly in some sense a tragedy. The character of Richard is deeply interesting, and he moves towards a tragic self-recognition cruder than but related to the self-recognition of another of Shakespeare's great sinners, Macbeth. It is notable that it is his personal qualities that receive the most direct attention; he is ambitious, like Macbeth, and having achieved his ambition, fear leads him to murder to protect himself. (Compare *Macbeth*, III.iv.136ff. and *Richard III*, IV.ii.63–4.) Like

Macbeth, who murdered sleep, who lacks the season of all natures, Anne tells us Richard sleeps badly. In both men we see the destruction of the self by an unbridled passion. Furthermore, Richard is especially branded with the personal sins of perjury and murder; their political reference, making him a regicide, a traitor, a usurper, is not particularly stressed. Unlike *King John, Richard II* or *Henry IV*, the play presents us with a usurpation without expatiating on the political sins involved in it. Furthermore, the issue of revenge – a favourite Renaissance moral conundrum – is very much present in the play, and is deliberately heightened by Shakespeare. The revenge play, a recognized sub-genre, clearly interested Shakespeare – after all *The Spanish Tragedy*, which turns on the issue of revenge, is one of the sources of *Richard III*. It is of the very nature of the revenge play that it highlights the problem of the relationship between private justice, public punishment and Divine Will. The central irony is that the revenger transgresses God's promise and prohibition, 'Vengeance is mine, I will repay, saith the Lord,' both to his own damnation and to the effecting of God's justice by becoming His tool. For example, in *The Revenger's Tragedy*, Vindice is consumed by a sense of injustice and of the corruption of the court, and determines to execute justice himself. But in so doing, he becomes, tragically, as bad as the thing he hates, and is himself justly destroyed at the end of the destruction he has wrought around him. Yet through him God's justice on the sinners has been done.* *Richard III* is not a revenge tragedy, but it is related to one: the characters of the play are virtually all tainted by guilt, passionately aware of the guilt of others and caught up in a tempest of hate. Richard, thinking he is serving his own ends, is being used by Providence systematically to clean up this world of blood by being an instrument of punishment; and in doing so he increases his own guiltiness and his certainty of damnation.

Finally, Shakespeare has used in this play all the techniques we associate with his tragedies: the insertion of non-historical scenes to develop a particular area – here, the philosophy of revenge; the insertion of supernatural events to suggest a divine vengeance operating to punish sin; the evocation of pathos in the death of children. As I shall demonstrate later, he chooses an appropriate Classical four-movement structure for it. All these are focused round a figure that dominates the play without a single break, whose ambition is its mainspring, and whose

---

* *Hamlet* is full of this issue: it is Hamlet's perception of the ambiguity of revenge that constantly stays his hand, and our expectation of the revenger's career that contributes so much of the irony to the action.

29

death, though utterly just, nevertheless leaves us with a sense of the loss of something which, however warped, was somehow extraordinary. Richmond's dullness, like Malcolm's, may be reassuring, but it is indeed dull.

Yet the play cannot not be a history too. The events are, after all, those in which the grandfathers of the audience could well have taken part; the play closes a long sequence of plays where the issues of legitimacy, of management of the state and polity, of the relationship between King and people are emphatically important. The sequence begins with the seizure of the crown by the house of York, and ends with its final loss. The Tudor victory was the basis of the political world the first audience lived in. Richard himself was a political model, as we have seen; he was believed in fact – fact that cannot be detached from his dramatic portrayal, whatever Shakespeare leaves out – to have been a committer of great crimes against the state – usurper, tyrant, offender against the common weal, who misused the cloak of public justice, administered by God's vice-gerent on earth, to conceal private revenge. Looked at from a longer perspective, his career was ironically worked by God's Providence in a way he had not intended, so that the sinners of the previous kinstrife could be cleared up, given their just deserts, so that Henry VII could start off with a clean sheet. So although Shakespeare did not (the epilogue excepted) include here any of the great speeches on political issues such as he gives to characters in the later histories, and such as he found in the *True Tragedie*, the play must be called a history as well as a tragedy.

The status of the play as hybrid is not paradoxical, but it is unusual, and may indicate something about Shakespeare's conception of the function of drama when he was writing it. It is perfectly possible, of course, that he did not use the political speeches in the *True Tragedie* because he felt that the historical context of Richard was so familiar and so topical that he could leave that dimension to be silently inferred; it is also possible that he wanted to explore in ways a straight-down-the-middle history might not let him the self-destructive nature of a human passion that was released from all moral bonds. But the answer may be a little subtler. It has long been known that Shakespeare drew heavily on several stories in the *Mirror for Magistrates* (see pp. 38, 40) for this play, and clearly read the book with deep attention. These stories are called tragedies, yet their purpose in that book is quite explicitly for political teaching. The play of the *True Tragedie* is similarly politically directed. The topicality of the figure of Richard that I discuss above might have suggested an idea of the play where the moral and ethical interest of tragedy became a necessary component in the understanding of truly political motivation. The play might then become the thing wherein the conscience of the nation could be caught. The ambitious overreacher would be warned, and chastened; his potential victims would be reassured of God's Providence.

4. The Use of the Sources

Many people feel some entirely pardonable impatience when it is proposed that it might be useful to look at the sources of a major work of art. After all, the argument might run, is it not the new building and its symmetry and efficiency that demands our attention rather than the old bricks of which it is built? We may be quite sure that Shakespeare's first audience did not run back for their copies of Lodge's *Rosalind* when they were going to see *As You Like It*. This powerful plea could be further strengthened by pointing to the way the enumeration of sources in a piece of complex writing can so easily become an end in itself that it disregards the alchemy that makes an entirely new thing out of old materials. To say where Shakespeare – or whoever – got something from can readily slip into evading the examination of what he has done with it in the total economy of the work.

Nevertheless, properly handled, the study of sources can be a very useful way of exploring what an artist's intentions were. When we can see the material from which he worked, it is almost possible to overhear his mind working, and the changes he made to the sources, as well as what he chose in the first place, may well help to confirm or qualify what we have felt, after looking at the work as a whole, to be his interests. It may also be possible for us to gain some idea of how the first audience would respond; it is after all highly material that Richard III is not just any old King that Shakespeare plucked out of English history to build a play round, but a figure already in the popular mind with an established set of references and whose career has a generally agreed area of meaning. Part of the interest will then become how Shakespeare engaged his audience in the examination of what they thought they already knew and understood.

We have to start by clearing the decks of the historical Richard. He ought not really to concern us in our present discussion, but something should be said of him since, for good or ill, Shakespeare's account has had a huge effect over the centuries on men's perception of him. First, it should be remembered that politics in the late Middle Ages was a pretty dirty and dangerous business, and few players of the game could remain of unsullied virtue. The stakes were high on all sides, and the elimination of adversaries by execution or even murder – the difference is slight – was often unavoidable. This is not said in any spirit of extenuation, for the morality of it was as clear then as now, but merely to get a perspective; after all, even the monarchs we most admire, like Elizabeth, had a good deal of blood on their hands, and her father and grandfather coldly and systematically set about exterminating any who could challenge their dubious title to the throne. Richard would have been a nonpareil if he had avoided this sort of guilt, and there is substantial and persuasive unanimity in the contemporary sources' imputing to him the murder of the Princes, and the judicial murder of Hastings and Rivers. He may have poisoned his wife; but he was not thought responsible for Clarence's death till later. (This is first tentatively suggested by Sir Thomas More.) He was seen as a usurper. But, on the other hand, there is good evidence that he was a very able soldier, a fine leader and politically not only astute but generous. There is even good cause for seeing the real villain of 1485 as Henry Tudor, and Richard as a man who had been deeply betrayed by men he trusted. His short reign is marked by a number of really substantial charitable benefactions, the beginnings of an attempt to tidy up long-neglected administrative and legal issues, and it is clear that when it was no longer to any conceivable advantage some at least of his towns and cities – like York – were prepared publicly to record their regret at his fall. But all this was forgotten. Over the years Richard, guilty as he was of some crimes, is assumed to be a natural home for all. His person – he was actually quite handsome – becomes hideous as an outward sign of his inner evil, and his overthrow is seen as a Providential seal of approval on Henry Tudor and his heirs. The traditional Richard Shakespeare inherited is a devil, and very far from the much more complex truth.*

Shakespeare was thus very considerably bound by the tradition of Richard. While he might have (indeed, one could argue, has) seen deeper into what such a historical personage might have been like, his audience's expectations would not allow him to run flat counter to them even had he had access to material that would modify the usual view. He had no such material. It would have been difficult for Shakespeare to have found much variation in the accounts of Richard's career and reign in historical accounts, for all the sources available to him about Richard are interlinked and draw ultimately on Sir Thomas More's *History of King Richard the thirde* (first printed, imperfectly, in 1543, but probably

---

* It is ironic that the very attractiveness Shakespeare gave his villain has led many who feel attractiveness ought to go with goodness to seek a 'historical Richard' who was virtuous. Josephine Tey's *The Daughter of Time*, one of the best results of this urge, is a delightful and clever novel, but should be regarded with some reserve.

written some twenty-five or more years earlier).* His account was incorporated into Richard Grafton's *A Chronicle at Large* (1569), and into Hall's *Union of the Noble and Illustre families of Lancastre and York* (1548). Hall also drew heavily on the careful work of Polydore Vergil, *Anglicae Historiae*, which began to appear in 1534; Vergil's researches in English history were well known to More, his colleague in Henry VIII's service. In time Hall was incorporated by John Stow's *Chronicles of England* (1580) and Rafael Holinshed's *Chronicles* (1577 and 1587).

Thus wherever Shakespeare looked for written material to back up the popular tradition of the demon King Richard, he could not avoid More's account of Richard. (He read it, in all probability, in Hall's *Chronicle*.) The bulk of his information as far as the flight of Buckingham, where More's account stops, is drawn from More; but More also suggested to him a treatment of Richard as well. More is more than a source, which only gives a man something to write about; he is a major influence as well, suggesting how the writing may be done.

More was only about eight when Richard fell, and thus could have had no first-hand knowledge of the events he describes. He got most of his material from Polydore Vergil, and Vergil's material came from something close to, or even from, the highly reputable *Crowland Chronicle*. His patron, Cardinal Morton, Bishop of Ely (who runs off to get strawberries for Richard in III.iv of Shakespeare's play) may have contributed some information; it would not have been favourable to Richard, as he was greatly employed by, and indebted to, Henry VII. More was a conspicuously honest servant of the Tudor house, and his history tries to demonstrate the hand of divine mercy in the establishment of Tudor rule after many years of political upheaval and civil strife – an idea glanced at by Shakespeare, as we shall see (below, p. 90). But he can hardly be a source of objective historical information about a defeated King who had a better claim to the throne than his vanquisher and successor; and like most Renaissance men he is, in any case, more interested in history as a moral and philosophical study than as the exact and dispassionate science the invention of which was still many years in the future.

More's model in the writing of his history seems to have been primarily the newly fashionable Roman historian Tacitus. Like him, he avoids a rigidly exact chronology: form is imposed on the raw material of events

---

* Ironically, we now know far more about the reign of Richard than Shakespeare ever could. The early sources, like the Chronicle of Crowland, or the diary of the diplomat Mancini, were not to be printed for many years to come, and the wealth of private letters and public records that bear on these events could not even be known about by a man of the sixteenth century.

by deliberately foreshortening the time-scale of the events of the reign of Edward IV in order to make them stand as a prelude to his real interest, the rise and reign of Richard. The gain in intensity is considerable, and the distortion of historical time allows him to seek out and express the moral shape of Richard's career.* Like every Classical historian since Thucydides, he fictionalizes details, fleshing out the bones of events with people's reactions to them and the stories they told of them. He invents well-turned speeches for his characters, using the decorous rhetorical register and structure for the situation: Buckingham's oration to the citizens to win their support for Richard as potential King is a fine example of the oratory of persuasion. The dying speech of Edward IV – so long and complex that we quite believe More when he tells us that after it 'therwithal the king no longer endur[ed] to sitte up' – is designed to act as a prophecy of the events that will follow his death if ambition – and we think, obviously, of Richard – breaks the bonds of kindred and affinity and religion that should hold the realm together. More uses it, too, to suggest the idea that in some sense the young Princes represent England, vulnerable to the dissensions of the nobles who must hold them in trust for the future. There is no serious attempt to make us believe these speeches represent what actually was said: they are what could credibly have been said, and introduce (especially in the case of Edward's) important ideas and themes which qualify our reading of the subsequent action. A good number of More's speeches are reworked by Shakespeare: More's account of the dispute between the Archbishop and Buckingham over the right of sanctuary is closely followed in III.i, and the verbal echoes of More in III.v, III.vi and III.vii are close. The dying speech More gives Edward IV, however, seems to have affected Shakespeare in a more profound way. It is, of course, the basis of Edward's dying attempt at reconciliation in the play; but its strong subtextual emphases on the idea of the nation as a family and on the need for the brethren to dwell together in unity (compare Psalm 133:1) if the woe is to be avoided that comes to a kingdom when its King is a child (compare Ecclesiastes 10:16) seem to have suggested to Shakespeare one of the important image-frameworks of the play: the family divided against itself, and destroying itself.

More's use of hearsay evidence (or straight invention) provides Shakespeare with a number of factual details not only for the treatment

---

* Shakespeare took this device even further, and disrupts the time-scale much more than More. The play has an extraordinary compression, and the events of some ten years seem to take place in a matter of days. (Cf. P. A. Daniel, 'Time Analysis of the Plots of Shakespeare's Plays: Part III, the Histories', *Transactions of the New Shakespeare Society*, (1877–9), pp. 257–346.)

of Richard – for example, his gnawing his lower lip when angry, his restless nights (obligatory for tyrants), his chronic suspiciousness – but also for such details as Stanley's dream of the boar (III.ii). There are also important areas, like More's extended, coolly ironic, account of the manipulation of the public Buckingham and Richard engage in, that he does not directly use: but those areas affect him in a different way.

For though Shakespeare's close dependence on material in More is very obvious, the influence is much more radical than merely that. More's book centres round the personality of Richard, and just as he handles events with the irony of a Tacitus, he handles Richard, and the response to him, with the satiric detachment of a Suetonius. Here is part of his first extended description of him:

... he was malicious, wrathfull, enuious and, from afore his birth, euer frowarde. It is for trouthe reported, that the Duches his mother had muche adoe in her trauaile, and that hee came into the worlde with the feete forwarde, as menne bee borne outwarde, and (as the fame runneth) also not untothed, whither menne of hatred reporte aboue the trouthe, or elles that nature chaunged her course in hys beginninge, whiche in the course of his lyfe many thinges unnaturallye committed. None euill captaine was he in the warre, as to whiche his disposicion was more metely than for peace. Sundrye victories hadde hee, and sommetime ouerthrowes, but neuer in defaulte, as for his owne parsone, either of hardinesse or polytike order; free was he called of dyspence, and sommewhat aboue his power liberall, with large giftes hee get him vnstedfaste frendeshippe, for which he was fain to pil and spoyle in other places, and get him stedfast hatred. He was close and secrete, a deepe dissimuler, lowlye of counteynance, arrogant of heart, outwardly coumpinable where he inwardely hated, not letting to kisse whome hee thoughte to kyll; dispitous and cruel, for euill will alway, but ofter for ambicion, and either for the suretie or encrease of his estate. Frend and foo was muche what indifferent, where his aduauntage grew, he spared no man's deathe, whose life withstoode his purpose ...

Even in this short passage – it continues with some juicy gossip ('as menne constantly saye') about Clarence's and Henry VI's deaths – we glimpse More's delicate use of hearsay, reputation and report: the public picture of Richard that so fascinates Shakespeare and, indeed, his Richard himself. But the really decisive thing that More does with the figure of Richard in his witty account is to make him not just a villain, but a witty and clever one, enjoying his game.* It is this that is the basis

* Later, in the Tower, in *A Dialogue of Comfort against Tribulation* (1534), More analyses at the end of Book II one sort of temptation against which Faith, Hope and Charity, and trust in Providence, will protect men: the *'negocium perambulans in tenebris'* – 'business walking in the shadows' of the Vulgate Psalm 90 (the translators of the English Bibles abandoned the reading *'negocium'* for a word meaning 'pestilence'). *'Negocium'*, More

for the extraordinary figure Shakespeare develops – a development that remains entirely true in spirit to the source Shakespeare used responsibly. Moreover, the domination of events by Richard in More's account, on the Suetonian model, may have suggested to Shakespeare that he conclude the account of the events of the Henry VI period with a play that would be not so much historical like the previous three but 'tragic' in its ethical concerns (see above, p. 28).

Other historical material, covering periods that More did not deal with, Shakespeare took substantially from Hall, backed up by Holinshed's second edition of 1587. But it is clear that the bare historical account has been imaginatively expanded and heightened, and that, entirely appropriately for a 'tragedy', Shakespeare has expanded hints or pregnant omissions in his historical sources by laying under contribution a large range of dramatic and poetic sources. The wooing of Anne, for example, is not described in any source; yet at some point, Shakespeare realized, Richard must have persuaded her to marry him, and the invented scene that resulted from this insight is one of the glories of the play (see below, p. 62ff). Similarly, chronology debars Queen Margaret from appearing in the histories; but without the historical memory, the long echoing colonnades of time she represents in the play, the ritualized litany of grief and crime of the Duchess of York, Anne and Elizabeth would be far less powerful. It has been demonstrated that Shakespeare is drawing here on Seneca's treatment of the women of defeated Troy in his *Troades*: an entirely happy choice of source, for despite the researches of Polydore Vergil, many people still happily accepted the bogus account of British history that would have it founded by Trojan refugees, and London 'New Troy'. Similarly, for the wooing of Anne, Shakespeare had only to make Richard interrupt the funeral of Henry at which he had made Anne chief mourner to provide an opportunity for a stunningly grotesque courtship over the corpse of bleeding England. The linguistic and dramatic model is again Seneca: the offering of the sword echoes the *Hippolytus*, and the wooing of Megara by Lycus in *Hercules Furens* suggests a way of handling Richard's suit and a style to couch it in. Moreover, the invention of this episode provides a beautifully ironic counterweight to Richard's apparently successful winning of Elizabeth's consent to the

---

explains, is the name of a devil tempting men to 'besynes' – to a covetousness of worldly things and power, a resultant loss of the sight of God and their eternal end. Those who succumb are not even aware they are being troubled and tempted. This throws an interesting light on his Richard, and is a strange anticipation of Shakespeare's, with his delight in 'bustle'. (Shakespeare could have read the *Dialogue*: it was printed in 1553, 1557 and 1573.)

marriage of her daughter, which is sketched in Hall and Holinshed. Surprised as he is at his own success in the first and too sure of it in the second, Richard's two wooings bracket his ravishment of England. The imaginative gain is enormous.

However, my original point, that seeing what Shakespeare made of his sources can throw much light on his intentions, is perhaps best demonstrated by examining the two dreams in the play and their relationship. Shakespeare had some warrant in his sources for Richard's nightmare before the battle of Bosworth – but none, of course, for the extraordinary expression of the divided self he gives him in his soliloquy. Clarence's dream, one of the finest and most theatrically effective pieces of writing in the play, is quite another matter. None of the historical sources even hint at it, and Shakespeare's sense of its importance in his play is indicated by the care he took over it. It has many ingredients: a major source, which it echoes in several details, is Thomas Sackville's 'Buckingham' in the *Mirror for Magistrates*, in which Sorrow leads the poet to the realms of the dead; there is a debt as well to the narrative by Andrea's Ghost in the first scene of Kyd's *The Spanish Tragedy* (1592). It echoes as well Ovid's *Metamorphoses*, in Golding's translation (1565–7), especially Juno's descent into Hades in IV.536ff., 604ff., and also the many descriptions of Hades in Seneca's tragedies – especially *Hercules Furens*. The heaps of treasure the sea traditionally conceals seem to be visualized in terms very like Spenser's description of the Cave of Mammon in *The Faerie Queene*, II, Canto VII. The whole thing belongs to a well-known genre of the dream-vision of Hell, ultimately dependent on the earliest accounts of all, in Homer, *Odyssey*, X and Vergil, *Aeneid*, VI. Yet the simmering of all these diverse elements of his reading, consciously remembered or not, in the limbeck of Shakespeare's mind has mysteriously transmuted them into an outstandingly coherent and sharply realized passage which though unnecessary to the narrative development is thematically and symbolically crucial to the balance of the play. It explores and illuminates the inevitable consequence – Hell – of Clarence's own guilt and at the same time ironically relates to his relationship with Richard.

The speech breaks into five movements. First, Clarence is dreaming that he has escaped from his imprisonment * and that Richard is partner in his delivery. (The irony of his trust in Richard needs no emphasis.)

---

* I am more than a little tempted here to suggest that Shakespeare, with consummate irony, is using escape from the literal Tower to suggest the old cliché of death releasing men from the prison of this world. There may also be a grim pun, considering Clarence's vinous end, on the Burgundy to which Clarence might plausibly have travelled if he left England. (Such a pun is made in *King Lear*, I.i.258.)

Secondly, Richard is (innocently) responsible for Clarence's falling overboard – from a Ship of State? – and drowning. The physical agony of drowning is preceded by the vision of the traditional treasure at the sea bottom, focused (literally!) in the striking picture of the jewels in the eye-sockets, which, like the bright jewels of a lady's eyes in conventional love poetry, 'woo'd the slimy bottom of the deep': the association of death, sexuality and gain hints delicately at the latter end of the unbridled desire for power and its symbol, wealth, which motivated Clarence and motivates Richard. And after 'death', Clarence knows no peace: in Hell he is challenged by those he betrayed and murdered, and is seized on for punishment by the fiends. The narrative of the dream tells us, as it were, what really does happen to Clarence after he is really drowned; an audience that knew of his end would see the grim ironic comedy of the speech. The speech leads him to a sincere recognition of his real guilt and his deserving of divine punishment. But even though he arrives at self-knowledge, he still fails to see through the arch-deceiver, Richard.

But Clarence's is not the only dream in the play. Shakespeare makes visible to us the dreams that Richmond and Richard have before Bosworth, and the reactions to these throw light on why Clarence's dream was elaborated at such length and with such obvious care. Richmond has 'The sweetest sleep, and fairest-boding dreams That ever entered in a drowsy head' (V.iii.228f.) – the sign of a good conscience. But he recognizes ('Methought' = 'it seemed to me', 1.231) that they are illusions, and emerges from them with a cheerful hope and words of practical wisdom. For Richard, on the other hand, the vividness of the dream forces from him a terrible recognition not of illusion but of what he *is*, a man divided against himself, whose real sins 'Throng to the bar' against him (200); in the mood and tense of that verb there is no escaping the reality of what his mind is doing to him. His dream forces him for the first time in the play to see himself as a man who is after all bound by the moral restraints he has deliberately overthrown, trapped in the prison of his own despair. But when we see Richard in this state, despairingly aware of his vulnerability to his inheritance of crime, we remember that the imaginative marker for this access of conscience and perception of the Hell that is in himself has been put down by the dream of his first victim in the play. Clarence's dream not only opens up the issue of guilt and conscience which are central to the play's moral scheme, but prepares the way for, hints at, Richard's sudden and shocking awareness of his very nature, his creaturely condition, fighting against what he has made himself. The later dream matches the earlier, and both together structurally enclose the play's major discussion of the perception of guilt.

The Induction is not the only thing Shakespeare read in *The Mirror for Magistrates.** It is difficult for us to realize now how original this work was, and how it might grip the imagination of an age. The Middle Ages had not left any dearth of writings about the Falls of Princes – Boccaccio's *De Casibus Virorum Illustrium* is a good example, and is used by Chaucer and by Lydgate. The emphasis on the fickleness of Fortune and the warnings against the pride that goes with high place were of obvious relevance to the great as well as of moral interest to their subjects. Where the *Mirror* (first printed 1559; a second part appeared in 1563, and it was expanded several times later) broke fresh ground was in making its material not conveniently distanced antique and legendary princes and great ones but the actors in English history of the recent past (Hall was the main source). It sought to use recent history as moral and political education, emphasizing that in the falls of nearly contemporary men as well as of past figures one sees the action of a just Providence punishing sin. This perception of the hand of God in human affairs is of obvious interest to a playwright like Shakespeare, who is deeply concerned with the morality of rule and kingship and its relationship to the divine *ordo*. It is also quite clear that on both sides of the political fence the book provided examples and arguments to advance polemic cases.

Much of it is fairly dreary verse; some, like Sackville's Induction to 'Buckingham', is rather good. Shakespeare clearly read the tragedies of Richard III, Edward IV, Rivers and Buckingham – pretty elementary research after all – but used three of them lightly and that of Edward not at all, so far as can be seen. His mind seems to have been delighted by some of the rhetorical felicities and the wit in the tragedies of Clarence, Hastings and Jane Shore, and a very considerable number of lines in the play echo, or even quote, lines in these poems. What the book seems to have provided, however, was not just verbal, but rather an attitude to the treatment of a historical subject that catalysed in Shakespeare's mind what he found in More and what he could see in contemporary stage practice.

For he was a sharp observer of his fellow-dramatists' work, and other plays are among the sources of this one. There is ample evidence, as we shall see, that the very concepts of the theatre, the playwright and the player intrigued him into serious thought about the nature of truth and of a man's true self *vis-à-vis* his role. Equally, he is aware that the illusion of the theatre is dependent on language and a delicate transaction

---

* 'Magistrate' here means a ruler to whom is delegated by God authority over his fellows on earth.

between the mind and consent of the audience and the players. Good ways of handling this problem could not be neglected; and Shakespeare clearly took useful ideas where he were found them. Marlowe's pushing of the idea of the villain who overreaches himself to the point where he is grimly yet unconsciously comic, but still terrible, where he is defiant in his damnation, has clear links with Shakespeare's handling of Richard, and it is no surprise to find many echoes of Marlowe's verse in the play. The characterization of (and the use of aside by) Barabas in Marlowe's *Jew of Malta* is frequently recalled by Richard; and Richard's overweening ambition would have been understood by Tamburlaine. Similarly, Thomas Kyd's use of the ethical conundrum of revenge as the basis of *The Spanish Tragedy* is highly relevant to the revenge-motif given to many characters in *Richard III*.

The dramatic handlings of Richard's reign outside Shakespeare bear witness to the strength of the tradition but have little organic effect on his play. The pastiche Senecan tragedy in Latin by Legge, *Ricardus Tertius* (c. 1579), though it circulated in manuscript, seems not to have been performed, and it must be doubted whether Shakespeare knew it. The material common to both is inevitable if both drew, as they must have done, on the same historical sources. The *True Tragedie of Richard III*, which exists in a poor printed version dating after Shakespeare's play, may well have been quite an early play which in all probability Shakespeare knew. But he seems to owe nothing to it. The *True Tragedie* concentrates very little on Richard himself and develops him hardly at all; some of its events, like Jane Shore's discomfiture, Shakespeare has deliberately left out. And in the study of sources, what is not used of what is available is as significant as what is.

The synthesis of the chronicle, admonitory, dramatic and poetic sources, into the unified play that we have is ultimately beyond explanation. But we can draw some conclusions to set beside those we have already reached about Shakespeare's interests. In the first place, the subsidiary falls of Richard's victims, of which the *Mirror* by its nature must, as they are free-standing, make much, are reduced in relative importance and poetic power so that we do not waste too much pity on them. Pathos is not the long suit of this play. Just when it begins to get going, we are reminded that we are wasting our pity on a criminal: the introduction of Margaret and her historical memory makes us see those various falls as deserved, as necessarily bloody exact justice for old sins, and thus their originator as an albeit unwitting agent of an inescapable Nemesis. This throws a lot of our attention onto Richard's manipulation of circumstance and, like an actor, manipulation of people's responses to himself – issues that bulk very important indeed in the scheme of the play. Moreover, the play is singularly devoid of episodes of penance and expiation, and the tragedy of Jane Shore in the *Mirror*, which deals with exactly that, and which Shakespeare clearly read (for he echoes the description of Fortune there in Anne's description of Richard (I.ii; and IV.i.79), is thus quite inappropriate to a play where the mercy and pity that such penance elicits is singularly lacking. But where, from this, we might expect bloody spectacle – and *Titus Andronicus* shows that Shakespeare was perfectly prepared to use horrific effects on stage when he thought it artistically necessary – from the bloodiest of English kings, we get not a single death on stage (except, perhaps, Richard's) – even Clarence is finished off offstage. (One can see the practical difficulties in the way of any other treatment in that case.) The conclusion that suggests itself is that the focus of Shakespeare's interest is on the complex figure of Richard as he manipulates the guilty through his own vastly amusing, amoral cleverness and their own desires, while all the time he is himself being slowly reeled in by a Providence that will not be mocked, even by Richard Plantagenet.

5. The Figure of Richard

Richard's voice and the power of his verse commands our attention from the play's first lines. That voice dominates our memory of the play. Until nearly its very end every serious initiative is his; all the other characters, even the perceptive Scrivener, define themselves by reference or attitude to him or his actions. The use of sources shows that Shakespeare saw him as the heart of the play, and we must now examine this complex figure.

Obviously, in the theatre his character is built up line by line as the play proceeds and, in analysing what Shakespeare has done with him, seriatim analysis has its uses. But before we can really get him into focus we need to look briefly at some of the prior expectations Shakespeare is deliberately tapping, besides just notions of Richard III as the Demon King, in the audience's mind. Especially we need to be sure we know in what ways the Renaissance concept of character, including dramatic, differed from ours, and we also need to look at the type of dramatic character that Shakespeare is building on.

It is a simple fact that Renaissance men did not think of the self in the way we do, and it is therefore highly improbable that when they came to write plays they suddenly used psychological and structural concepts that were not to be invented for very many years. When we watch a Renaissance play, we obviously cannot un-think completely what we now take for granted, but judicious and alert use of evidence not only from plays but from other types of writing, from the visual arts and from the design of houses can help us.

The sort of houses a society builds betrays assumptions about the idea of the family and of the self. Lines of cheap, back-to-back houses in a Victorian industrial town imply a view of man as an interchangeable unit of labour, whose individuation is of little interest. Modern tower blocks, or estates, equally impose restrictions on the type of life that can be lived: man is seen as a statistic to be accommodated, a consumer like all the others, to be persuaded certain material attributes of well-being are necessary; the physical forms of the flat or house forces the family to be nuclear, near the statistical norm (or there are impossible strains on the house as a machine for living in), and has virtually killed the great and humane and immemorial benefits of the extended family – with accompanying social problems of appalling magnitude. Both these types depend ultimately on a view of man primarily as an individual or as a unit in an economic process. Renaissance architecture and art shows us a very different idea: the houses that have survived, the treatises on good living, the pictures that calmly gaze out of time at us, all imply the essential publicness of a man's existence, and that that existence is intimately linked with a diverse community. The great houses as structures imply an amount of ceremony and distance in even the most intimate parts of one's life – at ablutions, or with one's wife – that seems most strange to us; the cottages imply a closeness of contact that would be intolerable without the mental walls of structures of authority. We should find most distressing the lack of privacy – and the consequent need for ceremony and ritualized behaviour – to which medieval and Renaissance men were accustomed. All this implies that a man defines himself by his role, that his life is governed by the obligations of that role, that his perception of his self-hood is against the background of a moral generalization of what is or is not appropriate – decorous – to an individual in his position.* A king has responsibilities, and temptations, and joys, that are not open to one of his subjects; a coal-heaver, as Aristotle is reported to have said, has some delights that are not decorous to a prince. In real life each would speak differently, and have differing perspectives on the world, and have different role-expectations; in drama, it is the simplest of all conventions that the low-life characters speak in prose, and even now we find it amusing when they attempt the artificiality of verse that on stage signals dignity and seriousness.

From the cradle to the grave men acted a part, more or less consciously. It was an age when in real life men and women explicitly adopted a role, with clearly defined expectations and obligations, and asked to be judged by how well they performed it. It was an age when this objectivity about the self could extend to the actual serious rehearsal of deathbed scenes and dying speeches, when life and death could be seen as arts to be studied and ideal models imitated. In addition to her role as 'Prince', the Queen consciously adopted as a political tool a 'conceit' that she fulfilled the role and persona of the virgin goddess Astraea, last of the immortals to leave the earth after the golden reign of Saturn, and whose return would herald a time of peace and justice. If we look at her portraits we see, indeed, a representation of her physical appearance; but when we have learnt to read the picture's signals and symbols aright, we see that she is being defined not as a person simply,

---

* Books of 'Characters', like Overbury's (1614), or Earle's (1628), which are a series of short essays on 'A Downright Scholar', 'An Actor' and so on, clearly imply links between decorous physical appearance, moral behaviour, social expectations.

but as a person in a role, which is in turn defined by the allusions to abstract, often moral, ideas of that role in the rest of the painting. She saw herself, indeed, as a walking symbol, and descriptions of, for example, pageants in her reign show us that her subjects consented in this fiction. We could so easily dismiss all this as a game, but it affected her personal life, the political life of the country, and the way men formulated their hopes and fears. Role models provide a political language and some of the standards of social morality. Self-consciousness in the role, the willing use of the role-model as a means of self-valuation, crops up everywhere once we are aware of it; in this play, we can see it not only in Richard himself, but also in Anne playing – quite genuinely – the role of mourner when she is interrupted by Richard, and probably too in the type of speech Richmond addresses to his soldiers – which belongs to a recognized and common family of such addresses.

But these examples bring us up against the problem of dramatic character. If role-playing – and a man may in his life play many parts – as a means of seeking and defining the real self is usual in real life, it follows that dramatic characterizations by author and actor will not only be determined by these preconceptions but invested with an irony we might miss. Role and its values will be major determinants in the writing of a character, the way he will be dressed, attended and move on stage, the way the actor will play him, and the way the audience will receive what he presents; but at the same time the audience is aware of the illusion of his performance of his 'personating' (to use the word and idea in vogue after about 1600) or expressing the real inner nature of the character.*

It is just where the dividing line between illusion and reality lies that worries Bottom in rehearsing the play in *A Midsummer Night's Dream*; it is precisely this issue and the response to it that bothers Hamlet when he meets the Player King. For an actor acting is also a man living, a real man suddenly acting another man who once was (or might have been) real. The illusion he creates gives rise to feelings that are real but may not be directed to a strictly real object. For Hamlet, here is the Player, on request, as a social grace, producing out of context a tragic speech. The implication of the request in the first place is that the Player's art is to be enjoyed, and is not to be mistaken for reality. He appears moved by it, so that the observer sees real tears, and all the signs of real feeling,

---

* It must not be forgotten that the craft of acting by which one achieved the illusion of reality was highly conventionalized itself, and we should probably find Renaissance acting very ham. There existed a formal grammar of bodily movements, gesture, position and facial expression as ways of conveying quite complex ideas systems, and this grammar provided a basic structure on which an actor could build his interpretation.

and begins to sympathize with those feelings. But the actor is not moved; he is employing his art, and is pleased if it moves others – his desire is to be praised for the skill with which he does it. So the relationship between the appearance of real sorrow, the result of art and the real thing – and the parallel between the man who appears to feel and act with no cause and Hamlet, who has cause but is unable to act or to orchestrate his feelings – become central; Hamlet sees the difficulty of coping with, knowing, genuineness of feeling – 'What's Hecuba to him, or he to Hecuba?' – and acting (in both senses) on it, while the audience is brought up sharply against the paradox of illusion, their non-illusory response to it, and the effect it has on them in real life in their own roles. For their lives do not stand still while watching a play.

Shakespeare, right at the beginning of his career, is addressing this issue in Richard. We are, obviously, watching an actor playing Richard, and admire his skill and criticize his interpretation; but we easily forget we are watching an actor playing a man who is self-confessedly and *par excellence* an actor creating an illusion exactly similar to the illusion we are watching. For Richard in the play is never what he seems; he is an actor role-playing to suit his purposes and his audience; he invites us to watch his histrionic skill; he role-plays and stage-manages so much that the conflicts between the roles remove any centre there might be and leave him as empty, a man of many voices, a divided self, whose only essence is his will. The first illusion he gives of enormous energy and life is shown itself to be an act, at the root of which lies the inner static despair of Hell. Richard is Shakespeare's first study of the problem of the Player King, and the first play where he explores the ambiguities of dramatic characterization. Moreover, the lack of physical distance between stage and audience – even the actual presence of the smart set on the stage and above it – makes the actor almost a member of the audience who is playing in a charade. For Shakespeare's audience, the stage was not a remote other place, but somewhere where men of their own community might strut and fret their hour upon the stage. The relevance – to use an overworked word – of the play to their own political and social and moral concerns is thus doubly inescapable; it can hardly not be a discussion and reflection of them, in however remote a time and place it may be set.

Given, then, that Shakespeare's concept of character in this play differs from ours largely by being governed by the notion of role rather than individuality, it follows that Richard's character is best approached through recognizing its dramatic type. Obviously, as he plays a King ideas of kingship and of the role of the King are – self-referentially –

present; equally obviously, the inheritance from the Moralities and Interludes (see pp. 15f, 48f) will control some of the conceptualization and handling of the arch-betrayer, schemer and villain. Without the Vice or comic devil of the Moralities we could not have Richard as he is; without the concept of the Machiavel we could not begin to explain him.

Discussion of Richard has to start from the soliloquies Shakespeare gave him in *3 Henry VI* III.ii.124–95 and V.vi.61–93. These are quoted in full in the Appendix to this book. The second anticipates in detail the murder of Clarence in the first act of *Richard III*; the first implies that before the earlier play was put into its final form Shakespeare had a pretty fully developed plan for the way he would use Richard, and a lot of the ideas in it are echoed more tersely and pointedly in the opening soliloquy in *Richard III*. Richard's ambition for the crown vaults over the difficulties to his succession presented by 'lustful Edward' and his probable progeny, his brother 'Clarence, Henry, and his son young Edward'; but moment-arily he loses hope, and determines ironically to seek out a 'heaven in a lady's lap'. Bitter consciousness, however, of his physical deformity leads him to dismiss this idea as impossible, and he returns to his ambition –

> whiles I live, t'account this world but hell,
> Until my misshaped trunk, that bears this head
> Be round impalèd with a glorious crown.

He sees himself fighting the difficulties in his way to it like a man hewing his way out of a thorn-thicket; and chillingly the idea of wholesale cutting and slashing contained in 'hewing' becomes a programme for murder:

> Why, I can smile, and murder whiles I smile,
> And cry 'content!' to that which grieves my heart,
> And wet my cheeks with artificial tears,
> And frame my face to all occasions.
> I'll drown more sailors than the mermaid shall;
> I'll slay more gazers than the basilisk;
> I'll play the orator as well as Nestor,
> Deceive more slily than Ulysses could,
> And, like Sinon, take another Troy.
> I can add colours to the chameleon,
> Change shapes with Proteus for advantages,
> And set the murderous Machiavel to school.
> Can I do this, and cannot get a crown?
> Tut, were it further off, I'll pluck it down.

The growing confidence of these lines closes in a chuckle entirely consistent with the Richard of the opening of the next play; but the relationship goes much deeper. The mermaid, fair seeming but with a foul and evil tail, luring sailors to destruction, was a standard image of the deceptiveness of evil. The marine idea is repeated: Clarence is totally taken in by Richard, dreams of being pushed overboard by him, and dies by drowning. The basilisk, a mythical animal that killed by its very sight, anticipates not only in general terms the fate of those on whom Richard's suspicious or ambitious gaze rests, but also ironically the wish of Anne that her eyes were 'basilisks, to strike . . . dead' the Richard who is courting her; he does play the public orator like silver-tongued Nestor, using the ambiguity of language to persuade; his private deceptions are as successful as Ulysses', and the Troy he takes is an England which under him is brought to witness the destruction of its entire ruling family.* The ironic self-reference in 'Change shapes with Proteus' is a climax to this catalogue of his power to create evil illusion, to dissimulate his nature and motives. But changing shapes also focuses all the hints – in 'artificial', 'frame', 'play the orator' (see p. 52) – of the actor who seems genuine but is all the time controlling his audience's response by his art of illusion. Richard in his play is a consummate actor who delights self-consciously in his effectiveness in whatever part he is playing; and he invites us to watch him playing it and share in his delight in his skill. Here is the first of the theatrical metaphors which are crucial to Shakespeare's portrayal of the deformed King, a King who is constantly presenting himself to us not only as actor but also as director in a play manipulating his victims. This sense of his own theatricality is a major aspect of his character; it also is designed to point to two major strands in his stage ancestry.

Richard and the Morality Vice

The Morality plays and their more secular descendants, the Interludes (see above, p. 15ff), were still familiar in the 1590s and later, and provided

---

* In the Middle Ages and later London was frequently called in romance 'Troynovaunt', or New Troy. So Richard's comparison of himself to Sinon, whose deceit caused the Trojans to drag the wooden horse full of slaughtering Greeks into their city, is rather more apt than it looks at first sight. The researches of Polydore Vergil, which demonstrated the falsity of the old account (the twelfth-century Geoffrey of Monmouth was very influential in its dissemination) that Britain had been founded by refugees from Troy led by one Brutus, did not remove this delightful notion from people's minds: Drayton's *Polyolbion* (1622) uses it, for example.

almost the only dramatic languages and techniques the new secular theatre had originally at its disposal. Author and audience expected them and relied on them as a means of analysis and communication. Just as writers for television drama in the 1950s took a long time to break away from the 'fourth-wall' convention of contemporary theatre and develop the sort of camera movement and use of close-up we now take for granted, the dramatists of the last quarter of the sixteenth century were having to find a way of writing that fitted their society and medium by building on and modifying the old dramatic formulas.

The dramatic methods the moralities used relied on the audience's assent to the presentation of human problems and conflicts in objectified allegorical terms: it was perfectly usual for characters to be called 'Mankind' or 'Good Deeds', and the interplay of such characters is therefore an externalized analysis of internal struggle. But man's moral struggle took place against the background of a cosmic struggle between the forces of Good and of Evil, and may well be ironized by it; and so the physical presentation of representatives of these forces is usual. The Devil goes about as a roaring lion, seeking whom he may devour, even while he knows that Christ's victory on Calvary has destroyed his own power for ever. Therefore he and his angels are ultimately comic, while not ceasing in any way to be dangerous. As they tempt mankind to turn away from the assured path of salvation, they must exhibit a deep attractiveness that, to be dramatically credible, must be felt by an audience; they must offer things that appeal to man's most powerful desires. But ironically their tempting of man increases their own damnation. Grim comedy, therefore, is a major element in these allegorical dramas.

But the moral interest and purpose of this type of drama demands that the audience draw the right lesson from it through their amusement, and therefore the actual happenings of the play have to be distanced to avoid too much identification. The names of the characters in the Moralities largely do this; and another device of major importance, which the dramatists who drew on these plays happily took over, is to 'frame' the events with a Prologue, or Epilogue, or Chorus, so that they become a *demonstration* of a general thesis. A fine example of this is in a play that has close links to *Richard III*: Kyd's *The Spanish Tragedy* uses just this Morality technique when it opens with the Ghost of Don Andrea talking to personified Revenge. Their conversation places all the subsequent action in an ironic frame; and as they are both from Hell, the ultimate resolution of the pattern of the plot, aesthetically satisfying though it may be, demonstrates once again the capacity of human beings to damn themselves through following their natural and understandable desires. Other plays of the 1580s and 1590s besides Kyd's use the morality technique of putting an allegorical cage, where the outcome is known, round the free choices of the characters. These frames, particularly when fully developed, as they are for example in the five dumb shows in *Gorboduc*, help the dramatist to draw a moral, to control incident, to provide exposition, to suggest pattern and meaning, and to provide a causal chain including the narration of incidents that could not be or were not chosen to be located in the represented action. The main devices used are the Prologue or Epilogue, the Induction, the dumb show and the Chorus. Shakespeare at some time or another uses all of these: in *Hamlet*, Hamlet is Prologue and Chorus to the play within the play, which is explicitly moral; in *2 Henry IV*, Rumour's opening speech provides a major thematic insight into the subsequent action; in *Henry V* or *Pericles* the use of a Chorus is crucial to the proper focusing of the events and our response to them, and in *Richard III*, Richard's opening speech, whatever else it does, invites us to see the action as demonstrative of the power of him who rejects all moral restraints, to share in his glee in that power – and at the same time provides an irony unperceivable by him, for even without our historical knowledge we know that a man who talks like this must, ultimately, fall into deep damnation.

But in glancing at Richard's opening soliloquy we touch on another method the Moralities and their descendants used. The framing of the morality drama by supernatural figures, comic to a greater or lesser degree, led to the development of one of the most enduring of dramatic figures: the Vice, who gradually acquires command over all the other evil forces in the play. The Vice becomes a central figure, the main vehicle of comedy, an amoral, unscrupulous, witty deceiver,* a mischievous trickster and manipulator, a solitary figure whose familiar address to them assumes the complicity of an audience – who know that ultimately he will slip on his own banana skins. He was the most vivid and amusing of all Morality figures, and survives long into the time when drama had become largely non-religious. The Vice is an

---

* As early as Prudentius' *Psychomachia*, personified Vices who deceive by disguising their real nature had been linked with the playing of an illusion by an actor. While the earlier Moralities do not use such disguise for the Vices, the secular plays that descend from them do – for example, Skelton's *Magnyfycence* (1530?) has Vices disguising themselves and playing the part of virtues the better to win men to their harms. The deception and disguise that is part of the very nature of acting and drama is obviously highly pertinent to the nature of the Vice, who is often made to use the terminology of acting in his speech. The self-reference can be crucial, as in the case of Richard.

embodiment of evil, and in the old drama his occurrence is perfectly explicable; but when dramatists break out of that overtly religious frame, they do not abandon a figure who is theatrically so effective and popular. This creates a problem, for once the religious or spiritual context is stripped away from him, the Vice's evil and his motivation become rationally inexplicable and have to be accepted as a mere *donnée*. The explanation of character motivation became a fundamental problem for the secular dramatists of the 1580s and 1590s, and particularly so in the case of the villain. Even after the extraordinary development, particularly in Shakespeare, of a dramatic language to express or suggest a coherent inner motivation for characters' actions, where what we see has the illusion of an existential reality from which we may draw the inferences we would in real life, many characters who descend from the comic manipulating Vice show that they are relying on their ancestry to explain their present. They remain symbolic and undeveloped in strategic as distinct from tactical motivation. Volpone's nature in Jonson's play is only explicable if we recognize the signals in his name – the Fox, a symbol of trickery – and in his opening speech, which indicates his personification of the Deadly Sin of Avarice; Iago's explanations of his motives are perfunctory and not at all convincing (as well as conflicting), and Othello's agonized demand for his reasons elicits only the response, 'Demand me nothing: what you know, you know' – there *is* no reason. Richard's 'therefore . . . I am determined to prove a villain' in his opening speech suggests a logical deduction and decision which on examination simply cannot be there; his malignity is motiveless.

These are real difficulties, particularly in a drama whose aim is to 'hold . . . the mirror up to nature' – however ironically that remark may be placed in Hamlet's address to the players within the play. But the advantage of using the Vice was real too: just as the interludes often gave him the job of explaining causes and linking events in the most vivid speech in the plays, so for Shakespeare and his immediate predecessors this self-explaining and self-complimenting figure allowed an integration of essential forwarding of the plot with bravura rhetorical comment upon it; he could also take over a lot of the functions of the Senecan tragic Chorus or the clever slave in the Latin comedies of Plautus and Terence who alerted the audience to what was going on. (The clowns, distant descendants of the Vice, retain some elements of this illusion-breaking address – even in Shakespeare, who does not use the device as much as his fellows did.) The medieval technique of direct address to the audience, a dramatic tool of some value, can more plausibly be located with him than with any other character, and the development of the dramatic soliloquy depends a good deal on this precedent – and even in its most sophisticated form, it never quite loses its importance as a moment when the represented time of the play's action is suspended so that we may see the action from a new angle.* Because he has been separated from his old context, he can be usefully combined at will with the types of figure the age was especially interested in: the Machiavellian schemer like Barabas in Marlowe's *Jew of Malta*, the clever but chilling misleader of youth like Falstaff, or the Senecan tyrant (see p. 75) like Richard III.

Shakespeare's conception of Richard clearly draws heavily on this background. His constant reference to himself as 'acting', 'playing a part' continues a major conceit of the Vice figures of the Moralities, who first gave such perfectly ordinary phrases unconnected with a theatre – for it did not properly exist – theatrical reference. Richard's dissimulation and playing of many parts, which More suggested, interested Shakespeare, and he gave him an ability to play with the ambiguity of language and discourse typical of such Vice figures as Haphazard, Ambidexter and Iniquity. Richard's aside at III.i.82–3 –

> Thus, like the formal Vice, Iniquity,
> I moralize two meanings in one word –

underlines this aspect of his cleverness and makes doubly sure that we understand how to take him. He is a man who plays roles: for example, the orator, as he promises in *3 Henry VI* III.ii.188; he can 'seem a saint, when most I play the devil' (*Richard III* I.iii.337); Buckingham tells him to 'Play the maid's part' with the Lord Mayor and citizens at III.vii.50. Like the actor with an audience, he deceives those who inhabit his stage world, while not taking in the play's audience; and while apparently being in control of his manipulations of himself and others, he is unaware of the fact that he is himself manipulated in his part by history and the dramatist. As a figure of treachery and evil, a specious deceiver, Richard has obvious links with Claudius, Edmund, Macbeth and Iago, but Shakespeare has given him, unlike them, a lot of references to the power the actor has to deceive an audience by the illusion he creates. The play

---

* Even when dramatists had developed techniques to the point where the main body of the play is completely self-contained, and the characters can ignore, as the Moralities and Interludes never did, the presence of a watching audience – a major step in the development of theatre as we know it – the Vice figure retains this custom of direct address to the spectators. Iniquity in the anonymous *King Daryus* (before 1568), or Haphazard in *Apius and Virginia* (before 1568) are examples. In Edwardes' much admired *Damon and Pithias* (1565), address to the audience (for explanation) is pretty well confined to the moments when the Vice character Carisophus and his pretended friend Aristippus are alone.

is filled, like *Hamlet*, with assertions of the actor's power. The words he speaks exist in a tenuous relation to the reality they purport to describe, and raise significant questions about the nature of theatre itself (see p. 99).

Our response to Richard again links him with the Vice. His soliloquy in *3 Henry VI* signals what he is, how we are to class him and by inevitable implication how we are to respond. He is doomed, because Vices always are, but not before he has caused havoc; he is highly attractive in his wit and his energy and his enormities of intent and performance are modulated by language to seem legitimately witty pranks we can thoroughly enjoy. Yet we never lose sight of the fact that here is evil personified: his ugliness of body, according to the usual Renaissance principle that outward shape ought to express inner nature, expresses his inner deformity; his portentous birth is a revolt against the pattern of Nature. Nor could a sixteenth-century audience forget that this man was the English equivalent of a Hitler or a Stalin, covered in the blood of those to whom he should have been as a father, who was destroyed by Providence when he thought himself secure. We are seeing the vilest of politicians and never forget it. For if we did not recognize it from his first speech in his own play, the soliloquy in *3 Henry VI* would have alerted us to the fact that he is a murderous 'Machiavel'. The background to this concept is so important that it needs a digression in description, for by using this conventional figure Shakespeare is able to get over a major problem in suggesting a credible motivation for the Vice.

The Machiavel

Niccolo Machiavelli (1469–1527) was a Florentine statesman, historian and philosopher, who in all probability would have been largely ignored except by scholars had it not been for a little book he wrote on the management of the state. *Il Principe* (1513) is undoubtedly the fruit of his deep researches into Roman history (especially the work of Livy), as well as an analysis of recent Italian history. It is an attempt to describe (and prescribe) how politics work in practice rather than how they should work in theory. The notion of an Order in the Universe which embraces and is mirrored in the human state (see pp. 7–8) is not so much rejected as ignored: Machiavelli is interested in providing a manual of effective political conduct for a modern ruler anxious to secure and maintain his position. (He is writing, of course, with particular reference to his idealistic desire for a ruler who would unite a divided Italy and drive all foreigners from its territory.) Conventional morality – justice, honour, mercy, truth, all the King-becoming graces Malcolm lists in *Macbeth* IV.iii.91ff. – are thrown aside. The sole criterion by which a ruler should govern is usefulness, and he sees the duplicity and intrigue by which Cesare Borgia operated as admirable because they were effective. The end justifies the means.

The book caused an outraged reaction: some went so far as to claim it was inspired by the Devil, and a crop of replies reasserted the old values. Some people, of course, only knew the original through the replies to it, but by the middle of the century translations were circulating, in manuscript at least, in most of Europe. Machiavelli's was one of those books that everybody professes horror of and reads under the bedclothes; his very name became an English noun, the Machiavel, signifying an utterly amoral, clever villain. The policies of a number of Elizabethan politicians – Thomas Cromwell, Cecil, Leicester – were influenced in some degree by his book, and Francis Bacon, Walter Ralegh and Christopher Marlowe all made some intelligent use of it, even if occasionally gingerly.

The horror arose not only from moral principles, but from a recognition that no system has a defence against the man who refuses consent to it. Machiavelli's ignoring of the obligations of Degree, and his making the will of the Prince the highest moral imperative, both fascinated and appalled. Suppose a man like Edmund in *King Lear* were to deny consciously all moral restraints on his conduct, all constraints of degree; suppose he were to gain real power, and make the gaining and keeping of that power his only good. Theoretically, the whole creation would turn on him and restore a just and holy equilibrium. But there had always been examples of men who had done just that, and who had survived; some, even, had turned out successful rulers. As Queen Elizabeth's godson, Sir John Harington, cynically put it,

> Treason doth never prosper; what's the reason?
> If it do prosper, none dare call it treason.

An uncomfortable thought indeed, which eventually would lead to the unravelling of the seamless web of the old world view. One of Shakespeare's interests in his history plays and tragedies is the testing of the validity of the model as a metaphor for how people behave politically. The question that will not go away is whether the model has any real existence apart from metaphor: whether it is not, in its moral application, just wishful thinking.

Machiavelli himself in the popular mind becomes a devilish clever villain, a playhouse Machiavel. The plays of the period are full of these amoral figures, outsiders, often at the start excluded from the hierarchy and order of the state, seeking to advance themselves to power by their wit and intelligence, but doomed to eventual failure as the forces of the Good they have denied reassert themselves – even if, in tragedy, the cost is appalling. Like the 'White Devil', a devil appearing in the likeness of an angel of light, they are actors, able to present to their victims an appearance of honesty and integrity that is completely convincing. 'Honest Iago' takes in Othello and everyone else, and the audience, who are not taken in by him, can see how tragically easy it is to be. Masters of attractive language and illusion like the Vice, they are articulate, often given moments of direct, almost conspiratorial, address to the audience, whose sympathy and agreement they are ironically made to assume. But they are rejectors of all the normal assumptions about the morality of human society, destroyers of anything that is good and noble, and the political Machiavels – Edmund, Richard, for example – work on the 'Machiavellian' principle that their own advancement and the keeping of it justifies any means from murder downwards. Moreover, the strength of this convention means that a dramatist has only to signal that there is a Machiavel in the house for a large part of the characterization to be already done: it is there in the audience's mind. As a result, awkward questions about motivation and background simply do not arise. For example, when in *Much Ado About Nothing* Don John in I.i. is virtually silent, cool and reserved in his acceptance of Leonato's belated welcome, we suspect trouble; and I.iii. confirms us in our suspicion that here is our self-declaring 'plain-dealing villain'. Or when Lady Macbeth has just read Macbeth's letter (I.v.), her first lines in this tightest of plays indicate that in her we have a female Machiavel whose own motivation is not our interest, while her effect on Macbeth is.

Shakespeare's Richard belongs therefore to a numerous family indeed; it includes for example Barabas and Mortimer in Marlowe, Bosola and Flamineo in Webster, as well as in Shakespeare Edmund, Iachimo and Iago.* So his determination to set Machiavel to school, and the bantering tone in which he says it, are crucial to an audience's recognition of what

---

* It is worth remembering that our first sight of Hamlet, a black figure self-excluded from the ordered visual pattern of a glorious court scene and commenting wittily on it, suggests a Machiavel figure. That ironic misjudgement is important in controlling our subsequent response to him.

A number of Shakespeare's later Machiavels are actually developed very interestingly: Iachimo and Edmund, for example, seem to express regret, genuine or not, at what they have done. No stock Machiavel would have been capable of such moral insight.

to expect from this figure and how to respond to him; and in *Richard III* those expectations are abundantly fulfilled.

But this play is rather a special case. Richard's victims are almost all made to be themselves steeped in crime and guilt, and what happens to them they have in fact deserved. Richard without knowing it is actually helping to purge the world of the evil of which he is the starkest representative. Thus here the audience has a double pleasure: they can enjoy his wit and cleverness, his diabolic intellect, even applaud him and laugh at what he does to his victims, in the knowledge that eventually the rug will be pulled from under him. The diabolic intellect is enjoyable and comic precisely because it is ultimately hoist with its own petard. They have the enjoyment of the evil intrigue without the moral soiling of commitment to it. Indeed, in this comic aspect, the play – however we label it – has a strong and important connection to something like farce. Obviously I do not mean here the 'who's doing what and with which and to whom?' romp through assorted bedrooms that we normally associate with that genre nowadays; the old English farce I am thinking of died as a genre centuries ago. The 'farce' of medieval satiric poetry and morality drama – the drama that was still available well into the 1580s and later – is a grim and cruel thing, with a large element of the grotesque in it. It is fundamentally moral. The style and presentation may be humorous; the purpose is not. In such poems as Skelton's *Tunning of Elinor Rumming*, written around 1500, the serious point about the debauching power of the ale-wife is made by writing a deliberately ugly – 'raucous' is Skelton's own word – comic poem about the slapstick grotesqueries of her customers in a world where all values but appetite have disappeared:

> Some wenches came unlaced,
> Some housewives come unbraced,
> With their naked pappes,
> That flippes and flappes,
> That wigges and wagges,
> Like tawny saffron bagges;
> A sort of foul drabbes
> All scurvy with scabbes . . .

Closer to *Richard III* would be plays like Jonson's *Volpone*, or Marlowe's *Jew of Malta*. Here the intrigue and discourse of the Machiavel figure, Barabas, have to be described as comic, but the playwright sees the evil in the fact and sees it intensely. The reaction is a double one: fascination and repulsion at the same time, an awareness of a terrible and absorbing misuse of reason in a world where goodness, simply by being good, is frighteningly weak. We are seeing just such a world with Richard bustling in it; as Machiavel he illustrates what happens to a world where the getting and holding of power and the impulse to Revenge (see p. 87) become the only values; as Vice, his delight in his own cleverness is infectious, his contempt for his victims justified. But it is a world that is almost Hell, and at the end the fascination evaporates and we see the reality of evil in Richard's realization of his own divided and contradictory self.

6. Richard's Performance

The element of this serious moral farce, even in a play that must be called a tragedy, is never very far from the surface. Without the humour that ironically plays round Richard and the wit and self-mockery he himself exhibits, he would be merely a monster, and no more interesting than any other.* We cannot avoid being interested, however, in the complexity of mind, the energy and the self-awareness evidenced by his self-mockery, particularly when our point of view at the beginning of the play is inevitably controlled by the attitude he, as a sort of impresario, suggests. At the end we cannot avoid feeling a sense of loss at the death and despair of someone so much more remarkable and self-aware than any other character.

The humorous cynicism with which Richard views the world is of a piece with that shown by the Bastard in *King John*. Both characters see through the pretence and the pretensions of the people among whom they move, and reveal that high words often conceal low motives. For this to be effective as a stage device, of course, some complicity with the audience in point of view has to be assumed; and that complicity is established by the soliloquy that opens *Richard III*. But the confidence that speech shows, and Richard's rise to the throne exemplifies, is something else again; it is a comic and hugely enjoyable perversion of what Castiglione in his *Il Cortegiano*† called 'sprezzatura'. In his dialogues Castiglione discussed the ideal courtier, who unites ethical, social and intellectual virtues, military and sporting prowess and displays these admirable talents with easy, confident grace. Richard shows just such an *élan* in his villainy and a delighted mastery of the roles he chooses to play. He is hero of his own play to himself.

My object in this chapter is to analyse the details of Richard's

---

* It is one of the oddities of Shakespearean history that throughout the eighteenth century and until Irving's Lyceum production of 1877, Colley Cibber's version of the play was performed to general approval. Cibber butchered the play of Clarence's dream, removed Queen Margaret and vulgarized the figure of Richard by destroying the delicate machinery for his evaluation that Shakespeare had set up. Charles Lamb, in a review in the *Morning Post* of 4 January 1802, was one of the few people who recognized that Shakespeare was not interested in monsters but in the witty and clever figure who misuses his great intellect whom he glimpsed in More.

† The book was translated by Sir Thomas Hoby in 1561, and was very popular in England.

performance in his play. Later, in Chapter Nine, I shall suggest that Shakespeare's perception of the ideas of tragedy I have discussed above (p. 20ff) led him consciously to model the form of the play on the four plot-divisions Renaissance critics like Scaliger posited of Classical tragedy – *protasis, epitasis, catastasis* and *catastrophe* (see p. 98). Richard's performance breaks into these four movements: his establishment of himself and his aims, the initial successes that follow his pursuit of power, the crisis in Act IV when he is no longer totally master of events, and the final slide to his defeat and death at Bosworth. The details I shall concentrate on here thus need to be seen in the context of a recognizable ironic sequence over which ultimately, whatever he might think and momentarily persuade us to think, Richard has no more control than an actor has over the playwright's plot.

Richard's first soliloquy demonstrates an immediately arresting command of witty, ironic rhetoric; he alludes in belittling and trivializing terms to the courtly Game of Love that was an admired part of accepted social behaviour – only to reject it (yet he plays it brilliantly with Anne); and over the whole programme of action he sets out for himself plays a self-confidence and grace that suggests total self-possession. His control of the initiative, from the wooing of Anne to the bamboozling of the Mayor and citizens, suggests the polish of the admired courtier in the person we should, from historical assumptions, least expect to find it. His charm and wit quickly elicit indulgent neutrality, if they do not win us to his side; a mere thirty lines is sufficient to get us very interested indeed, and to place in our minds the extenuating suggestion, as Dr Johnson noted, that his deformity is the cause of the wickedness he confides to us. But if we fall for this, we are falling for Richard's presentation of himself just as his victims in the early part of the play do. For set aside the beguiling rhetoric and the apparently logical process of I.i.14–31 is seen to be fallacious in its conclusion; the deformity is the outward expression of the inner *determination* to wickedness. We might make the extenuation, but Richard himself is using his ugliness merely as an excuse (that we can fall for if we like) for what he wants to do. (One might compare the casual and contradictory motivation Iago suggests for his actions.)

The speech functions exactly like an Induction or opening chorus framing what we are about to watch, establishing an ironic perspective for the majority of the play's action. It even sounds like an Induction at first: the high style of the first lines sounds like a congratulatory public address before a pageant. The clichéd image of storms past recalls the hoary equivalence of storm/civil war, and the self-congratulatory tone must be disquieting when we recall who is speaking. Soon that disquiet is increased: the rigid, formal conceits in ll. 5ff. begin to sound a little hollow when the adjective + noun/verb/noun structure intensifies in three parisonic antithetical lines (6–9) into adjective + noun/ pronoun/adjective + noun stressed by an alliteration, the balance of which suggests a hidden, contemptuous chuckle. The rhythmical rigidity begins to sound sickening, the rhetoric is sounding too contrived and formal to be taken at face value: more like parody of the high heroic style than anything else. The artificial and clichéd personification of 'Grim-visaged war' is suddenly quite indecorously 'capering' (splendid verb), and the sonority of the lines climaxes in bathos on the liquid sounds and lightweight ideas of 'lady's chamber To the lascivious pleasing of a lute'. (Richard's dislike for music – cf. the contemptuous alliteration of 'weak piping time of peace' – is a clue to his nature, that rejoices in discord.)

The contempt in line 13 undercuts all the apparent seriousness of what has preceded it. It is only at this point, when the expected and natural reaction to the cessation of civil war has been torpedoed, and that war itself made to seem much more manly and interesting than what has followed it, that Richard turns to himself. His rhythms become more urgent, and their onward impetus ceases to be contained within a couple of lines; the balanced sonority disappears in a much quicker, nervous tone, and the suspension of the conclusion of the sentence for twelve lines gives a sense of heightening tension and gathering interest. The sentence in ll.14–26 is a remarkable tour de force of rhetorical control. Three clauses emphasizing his ugliness are hung on the repeated pronoun 'I'; the first is relatively mild in tone, yet the physical appearance of Richard underlines the grotesqueness of the idea suggested, and the way the clause is phrased suggests less interest in women than in watching himself perform with them. This self-regard intensifies in the second clause: the wanton ambling nymph – a pretty contemptuous description – is less conceptually or syntactically important than Richard strutting – can a lame man strut? – before her, and in the whole clause is a hint of the mocking contempt he feels for a brother, now King, who employs his majesty just to be lascivious. (Notice how he harps on this to the Mayor and citizens later.) The third clause employs the rhetorical figure of climax to bring the whole movement to an emphatic conclusion. It is three times as long as the other two, concentrates on a rapid succession of adjectives and adjectival phrases stressing physical deformity, before closing on how Richard appears to the dogs. (When we remember the animal images applied to people in this play later, one cannot help wondering whether those dogs are just dogs, or whether they have coats of arms.) After this enormous preamble, the structure of the main clause resumes with the idea of Richard – again! – looking at himself, looking at his grotesque distorted shadow. Indeed, he is using the ugliness of his body as a theatrical prop. And when we look at other Induction speeches preceding plays of the period, like Revenge's in *The Spanish Tragedy*, the unusual nature of this one is obvious: instead of directing the audience's attention to events and persons distanced from the speaker, Shakespeare has used Richard to act physically to direct our attention to himself as a phenomenon and his acting in the plots he has, like a playwright, laid.

For, ultimately, the focus of interest in the speech is Richard himself. It shows a self-consciousness, a peculiar objective awareness of himself, and a perception of the events of the world round him only as they affect him. In 11.14–26 other creatures exist only in relation to him performing before them – he almost suggests performing before himself – and here is the first hint of that self divided almost to non-being that is most explicit in his nightmare before Bosworth (see p. 75). He is role-playing in his mind even when he rejects the roles he plays; he goes on to assert he will role-play a role he likes: a villain. About the only thing Richard is saying about his real self is that he plays roles; he is defining himself as a shapechanger. And that is exactly what he is in the subsequent action: the actor *par excellence*, until he can act no longer.

This speech is enormously engaging in itself. The wit with which it is said and the attractive contempt it implies (and assumes in the audience) for every other historical personage in his world win an initial indulgence – it is not exactly sympathy – which is used to the utmost. Richard swings straight into action; he takes Clarence in completely with a skilfully feigned blend of brotherly affection, confidential tut-tutting agreement about the Queen and Jane Shore and indignation at Edward's behaviour. His speech is courteous, head-shakingly sympathetic, saying what Clarence wants to hear. It is only in the ambiguity of lines like

> O, belike his majesty hath some intent
> That you should be new-christened in the Tower

that we glimpse the Richard we have just had addressing us. Richard is enjoying the joke with himself; and later, at 108ff., when Clarence seems to be included conspiratorially in the contempt for 'King Edward's widow' – the King is not yet dead – he seems to be promised a deliverance very different from that Richard supplies. The meeting with Hastings that follows immediately shows another of Richard's chameleon roles:

his attitude to Edward is inconsistent with the attitude he implied to Clarence, and here he chooses a moralizing piety:

> Now, by Saint John, that news is bad indeed!
> O, he hath kept an evil diet long
> And over-much consumed his royal person.
> 'Tis very grievous to be thought upon.

The two episodes demonstrate neatly that in a world where men have to proceed on the assumption that things are more or less what they seem and can only understand speech as what it seems to mean, Richard's exploitation of verbal ambiguity and mastery of self-presentation give him an enormous and – at least in the short term – unchallengeable power over other men. We could ourselves be taken in had we not seen the two meetings together, framed at the beginning and end of the scene by witty and engaging and amoral soliloquies.

This scene shows he can dominate and control those who think him their friend; the next one shows how by playing the unexpected role he can dominate his most implacable enemies. Dr Johnson found it especially tasteless. It is; Shakespeare, who after all chose to include it without any historical warrant, underlines that tastelessness by having Richard himself draw attention to the grotesqueness of his plan:

> What though I killed her husband and her father?
> The readiest way to make the wench amends
> Is to become her husband and her father,
> The which will I – not all so much for love
> As for another secret close intent . . .

(I.i.154ff.)

The parallel phrasing of 154 and 156 underlines that tastelessness and Richard's own bloodiness; moreover, it is stressed again in almost the same phrase at I.ii.230 when he has achieved his aim. The very situation is a farcical grotesque: the corpse of a murdered King, attended only by Anne, rudely interrupted in its progress by the man responsible for the death of Henry and Anne's father and husband; and then a public wooing (tasteless in itself) culminating in a betrothal in front of the murdered corpse.* Richard's ardent wooing in dazzling hyperbolic language is undercut by our knowledge from I.i.157 that it is mere talk – but talk that conveys to the hearer a fake reality she comes to believe in even though she ought to know better:

---

* The giving of a ring at 204–205 before witnesses (the silent bearers) would for Elizabethans constitute a legally binding betrothal.

> Your beauty was the cause of that effect –
> Your beauty, that did haunt me in my sleep
> To undertake the death of all the world,
> So I might live one hour in your sweet bosom.
>
> (I.ii.121ff.)

The brilliance of Richard's language and the resourcefulness of his wit in playing the role of lover are no excuse for Anne being taken in by a display of acting: the evidence of what Richard is and has done is there beside her on stage, and if we examine how Richard gets round her we see that in essence it is by appealing to her self-esteem, her idea of the power of her own beauty. Flattery, in a word.* Thus Anne shows not only a willingness to believe what is unbelievable but also a moral fuzziness that precludes us feeling any deep sympathy for her. Moreover, her grief in the opening lines of the scene, including the curse that she heaps on Richard, is histrionic in the extreme. The curse may be fulfilled – and indeed it rebounds on her later – but one can hardly escape a sense that her excess of language and deliberate flouting of public opinion in this display of grief when Henry is only being accorded 'maimed rites' shows a self-consciousness that also amounts to playing a part – and almost enjoying it. Anne is a victim, but she is at least in part a willing one, and in Richard's manipulation, and linguistic wrongfooting of her through fluent movement from rapid stichomythic exchange to soaring extended hyperbole, from the deployment of the language of conventional love poetry to the bluff-calling on kneeling and offering his breast to the sword he gives her, our interest stays with him and what he will say and do next. She engages hardly any sympathy. She does not really matter to us as a person, any more than Clarence does. What does interest us is how as an audience she is being taken in by a man we know to be acting a part. (Later, when she recognizes the fulfilment of her curse on herself (IV.i.65ff.), she sees she is 'captive to his honey words'.)

There is a particularly interesting exchange which illustrates this at 196–206. Formally the precedent for a rapid half-line stichomythia may

---

* He tempts her, significantly, exactly as the Devil tempted Eve – an echo Shakespeare seems to want, if we take Anne's words –

> Foul devil, for God's sake hence, and trouble us not
> For thou hast made the happy earth thy hell –
>
> (I.ii.50–51)

as alluding to the Fall. Cf. Elizabeth's recognition that she is being *tempted*: 'Shall I be tempted of the devil thus?' (IV.iv.418).

well be found in Seneca; but precedents do not explain the peculiar effect it has. The eleven lines, mainly six-syllabled and so not truly half-lines, read very like the common form of altercatory love song between a lover and his lass, the one promising his fidelity, the other being properly reluctant. Suggestion of this conventional situation is of course ironic – for Richard later disposes of Anne when he has no further use for her. But it is also highly significant for the way Anne has been drawn into playing the game on Richard's terms: meshed into creating with him the illusion of a love poem. Moreover, this speaking of a poem between two voices is something Shakespeare does elsewhere: when Romeo and Juliet meet they speak a formal love sonnet to indicate not only that they two have come together in the unity of a single poem, but also the depth of their feeling, and how it may be categorized; when Richard II is being parted from Queen Isabel, again they speak a reciprocating litany whose antiphonal tightness suggest the enormity of their division into two separate selves. Clearly Shakespeare is using this short passage in a similar way: to indicate the success of Richard's gulling of Anne so that in the end she is a willing partner in her own destruction. Moreover, the semantic emphasis of the first part of the passage is on the problematic relationship between speech, appearance and reality, and Richard here plays with Anne with an irony almost beyond analysis. She doubts his truth; he says that his heart, his inner nature, is to be guessed at from his speech. Richard is indeed 'true' as any man in this, for he has in wooing her confessed to all the crimes she accused him of; yet the flattery of saying they were done for her love has allowed her to forget that. And we, who know Richard for what he is, can see that in the *use* of speech, as here, to deceive Richard is indeed true to what he is – his truth consists in being false. The final implication is that of course Richard is a false villain – and virtually everybody else in the world of the play is so too: which is borne out by events. He uses exactly the same sort of linguistic technique later with Elizabeth – though there are very important differences between the two scenes – and, as with Anne, lets his contempt for her show as soon as he is left alone. But in that later scene the actor is deceived by another's acting: Elizabeth, despite Richard's overconfidence in his skill, is not playing his game (see below, p. 73f).

Acting is precisely what Richard's next soliloquy, chorus-like, calls us to applaud (I.ii.227ff.). He exults in overcoming the outrageous difficulty of the task he set himself, enumerating what was against him – family feeling, grief, revenge, conscience, divine law, his ugliness. But one cannot avoid the idea that his real feeling for Anne is contempt for someone so easily swayed, who so easily forgot a man Richard admits to be far his superior (and whose virtues make Richard's remembered crime the more horrible). But it is not primarily Anne he is interested in; it is once again himself. With a neat return of the ideas of the opening address to the audience, he thinks himself ironically a marvellous proper man; and once again the conceit of the looking-glass suggests that Richard's real focus of interest is his own prowess, his real emotion a deep interest in a self he is creating. In 254–5 the syntactical implication is of a Richard who judges the Richard who acts; in 262–3 the looking-glass provides a means of seeing himself as others seem to see him: in action.

These early scenes show Richard acting different roles whose only consistency lies in their being framed by addresses to an audience that is treated as admiring shadows in Richard's looking glass. They exemplify that perverted sprezzatura I have suggested is a major factor in Shakespeare's presentation of him. But they also illustrate the power of the White Devil (see p. 55) to deceive by appearing to be what his victims understand as 'good' and saying what they want to hear. That effectiveness casts some ironic light on the moral values of the victims themselves.

Richard is, however, aiming at the crown, and the crown is not won by bamboozling individuals in private. He has to act in public: both in a group and, in the important matter of controlling public opinion and support, to a group. Up to the point where he is actually King, his strategy is threefold: he seizes and keeps the initiative, so that he is constantly doing and saying the unexpected; he chooses and dictates the terms of discourse, adopting a persona and a linguistic register that engages his interlocutor on his terms – be it the hail-fellow-well-met friendliness to Clarence's murderers, the passionate Marlovian lover to Anne, the aggrieved and honest man at court, or the indulgent uncle with the Princes. Finally, he creates for himself an outrageous public mask of sanctity so effective that only with total knowledge of his actions can it be certainly distinguished from the real thing – even by those who should know better.

In the opening of I.iii the distressed Woodvilles, expecting the King's death, show a perfectly understandable fear of Richard: as the Queen says, 'A man that loves not me, nor none of you.' When Richard enters with Hastings, he is playing yet another role: the bluff man of good will, who has been cruelly misrepresented as an enemy because he 'cannot flatter and look fair, Smile in men's faces, smooth, deceive, and cog' (47–8). If this were indeed the case his anger would be justified; and he uses the illusion of that anger to provide an opportunity to insult the very people to whom he says he is friendly (55, 61, 70ff.). The torrent of rapid questions and the momentum of Richard's speech almost totally precludes effective defence against it: and the questions really boil down to the 'Have you stopped beating your wife?' type. Each of the Woodvilles in turn comes within range, and it is hard to feel any sympathy with them. When Margaret (of whom much more later, p. 90ff) enters, unseen, her hatred for all the quarrelling pirates has the authority of long experience of them, and her desire for revenge suggests a strict justice that must eventually be executed. For a few curious moments we have a point of view of Richard that is double-focused: he is what Margaret says (133) he is, and just for a moment we see clearly and objectively his moral enormity as well as enjoy the skirmish he is engineering. When she comes forward, it is Richard she first attacks; and he pays her back in her own coin, suggesting that her guilt deserves her sorrow (the mock piety of 181 is developed later). But even Richard is for a time silenced by the sheer cumulative force of Margaret's rolling up the catalogue of past crimes into the grand curse she delivers. But he still has a trick left; he is a master of timing and knows how it affects tense moments in the theatre. She works it up to a fine climax in the anaphoric and parisonic lines 227ff., suspending a huge structure of hate and accusation on the expected name 'Richard' – and with an insouciant timing Richard speaks her own name. That the moment is comic cannot really be denied; she collapses like a pricked balloon, even asks to be allowed to continue her curse properly, and Elizabeth seems to smile and share in the joke. Although Margaret tries to get up steam again, after this her fury is much less effective. The Woodvilles turn on her, and Buckingham displays not awe but embarrassment. The almost silent Richard restricts himself to sardonic comments, casually suggesting that he is paying scant attention (294). And when she goes out, those she has cursed – her curses are fulfilled in detail, and everyone cursed remembers it in the moment of their fall – dismiss her as mad.

In our memory, the scene is dominated by Margaret, the embodiment of past wrong, and Richard, the embodiment of its present fruit. These two relate very much in the way the parts of the first sentence of Richard's first soliloquy relate: the high seriousness is undercut by bathos and comedy, but they form part of the same whole. The clash between Richard and Margaret sticks in our minds, for the challenge does not go away: we know things catch up with him, even though Richard is able to turn the attack aside for the moment. His mastery of the initiative by timing, by saying and acting what others do not expect from the man they fear but would expect from one who shares their values and assumptions, is a major part of his control of situation; another factor is that his opponents have to respond to him transactionally, on the terms he offers to them in a given situation. When in II.i the dying Edward is seeking to do what a good King should, and reconcile enemies to each other, Richard approves this making 'peace of enmity' (51) and pretends to seek friendship with the Woodvilles. Again, because this line of conduct is one which societies for their own survival have to accept as plausible, they fall for it; and in the false glow of reconciliation Richard is able to drop the bombshell of Clarence's death (the fulfilment of his first plot) and imply the Woodvilles are responsible. The technique is the same as in I.iii: to use the suggestion of an honest desire for reconciliation as a way of causing further strife and advancing his own position. In II.ii, after Edward's death, his condolences to the Queen (101ff.) are unable to be distinguished by the recipient from the genuine thing; his kneeling for his mother's blessing as a good son should traps her who earlier had seen him as 'one false [i.e., deceptive] glass' mirroring her shame (52ff.) into giving it. It is only the audience, who can recall Richard's cruel joke to Clarence in I.i.109, who hear Richard's aside at II.ii.110–11 – almost a conspiratorial wink – who are aware of the delight with which he is playing his part and manipulating situational response to him. He enjoys the self-referential finesse of warning Prince Edward as any good counsellor of a Prince should about the dangers of appearance in III.i.7ff., of the 'world's deceit', the 'outward show' which 'Seldom or never jumpeth with the heart' where 'poison' lies. And, as a good actor should, he maintains his self-control even when Prince Edward, with the usual perspicacity of Shakespeare's children, is not convinced of Richard's good faith, and he and his brother, the only victims of Richard who are wholly innocent, taunt their future murderer with their suspicions of him (100–150). The ability to dissimulate and to 'personate' is central to Richard's strategy for winning the golden fee.

Richard's soliloquy at the end of I.iii (323ff.) functions like the soliloquies at the end of the previous two scenes: it uses what we have just seen as an example of method. We have seen Richard acting to individuals, and now we have seen him manipulating a group:

> I do the wrong, and first begin to brawl.
> The secret mischiefs that I set abroach
> I lay unto the grievous charge of others.

His cleverness is that his enemies and future victims are tricked into urging him to take the next step that he knows, and they do not, will advance him to the crown. It is the last extended soliloquy we get, or need, for some time, for once the parameters of Richard's performance are set up, the interest lies in watching him 'bustling'. And at the end of the soliloquy the crucial tactical device of his performance is made manifest:

> But then I sigh, and, with a piece of Scripture,
> Tell them that God bids us do good for evil;
> And thus I clothe my naked villainy
> With odd old ends stolen forth of Holy Writ,
> And seem a saint, when most I play the devil.

It is a truism that the devil cites Scripture to his own purpose, and can appear in the likeness of an angel of light. But Shakespeare makes Richard say this cliché in a much more interesting way than usual: the idea of clothing suggests something not integral to the person, the clothing is itself of rags and should not deceive, the verb 'seem' is balanced not by 'am', which we expect, but 'play' – even devilishness is an act for Richard, an act for which he needs the props of clothes and the sign-systems of gesture. The hints lying at the heart of this short passage reinforce the suggestion in '*determined to prove* a villain' (I.i.30) that there is no real Richard, not even a villain, who can be categorized and quantified: only a massive ego and a massive vanity. The fruition of this hint is in the soliloquy of Richard before Bosworth, where the self is divided into nonentity and the only reality left is the temporary role demanded by the immediate situation.

The main tool Richard uses in his developing plan is the appearance of virtue. What we can see as sanctimony is the beginning and end of Richard's created character. Richard's complicity with us allows us to see his delight in this outrageous masquerade that looks like real virtue to all the other characters except Buckingham. He controls his language carefully to foster this impression: his oaths are mild in an age that prided itself on their originality and resource and he constantly suggests or implies an appeal to Christian standards and God's law. An important early hint of this sanctimony comes in I.iii.179, where he suggests that Margaret is being punished justly for her crimes;* the same suggestion of the hand of a God he does not believe in operating in the politics of England is made in II.i.140 to divert the blame from himself. His clever hypocrisy enables him to fool everyone in III.i into thinking he desires peace; and he enjoys exploiting the ambiguity of language to laugh up his sleeve at those who fall for his surface meaning:

> Thus, like the formal Vice, Iniquity,
> I moralize two meanings in one word.

(III.i.82–3)

* Note that Richard does not imply here any motive of revenge in himself.

The best example, however, of his performance is when he and Buckingham act out their charade to the citizens. The mock-virtue that has been seen so far as one detail of Richard's political operation is here brought out into the open to be presented, as it were, as a memorable icon of its dangerous deceit. In all his political plays Shakespeare is careful to remind us that public opinion is an essential term in the problem of rule, and that the true King has to be King of all the people and enjoy their consent. To see the charade of III.v and III.vii merely as comic, therefore, is to miss its great importance as a demonstration of how popular support can be manipulated and gulled.

The citizens are not stupid. In II.iii they are fearful and suspicious, and know that 'full of danger is the Duke of Gloucester' (27). In III.vii they are notably unresponsive to Buckingham's warming up, and the Mayor speaks only three lines, the first of which could be construed in many ways from disbelief to admiration (III.vii.94). The little scene with the Scrivener (III.vi) shows that even a lawyer can recognize something pretty dirty has been afoot in the execution of Hastings. Yet Richard needs the support of the citizens to give colour to his assumption of the throne, and as representatives of the people of England they are the country he must rule.

Before III.v, Richard has trapped the overconfident Hastings into incautious protest against his apparently hysterical imputation of witchcraft against the Queen and Jane Shore, and used that hint of opposition to him to get rid of him. It is the first point in the play where Richard can deploy power openly, and it is notable that although the technique of surprise and hurt anger is used once more, he takes less trouble to conceal what he is doing. But he still needs a show of legality and some public support. At the opening of III.v Richard and Buckingham are discussing the technique of acting: the pacing of speech, the control of gesture and expression – how best to simulate to an audience. They are already dressed up in the sort of armour a timid man of peace would grab in panic-stricken fear. Before the Mayor they both pretend terror; and when shown the head of Hastings, Richard melts into elegiac mourning for one he loved. Yet in those speeches of mourning he is careful to suggest to the Mayor that he approves of values like trustworthiness, chastity and the due process of law. The Mayor is tricked into approval of the execution, and then Richard sends Buckingham after him to 'play the orator' (94) and, again, appeal to values the citizens must approve: lineal succession, hatred of tyranny, chastity. Delicately, too, this appeal is to play on past fear: fear of arbitrary power, fear of the power to debauch the citizens' womenfolk. And while

Buckingham is doing this, Richard will set the stage for his *pièce de résistance.** Buckingham's errand, as reported in III.vii.1–41, did not have the desired success: the citizens were 'tongueless blocks'. The persuasion of the orator has to be trumped, therefore, by the illusion of the stage. Buckingham manages Richard (44–54) exactly as a producer; the dialogue is partly planned, and Buckingham plays his part when the Mayor and citizens arrive in drawing attention to the difference between Richard's saintly and ascetic virtue and Edward's dissolute sexuality. (The cleverness of this ploy is that at least in part the attack on Edward is justified, and as a result the whole speech could seem plausible to the unwary.) Richard's appearance 'aloft' between two bishops elicits from Buckingham an interpretation of this visual picture:

> Two props of virtue for a Christian prince,
> To stay him from the fall of vanity;
> And see, a book of prayer in his hand –
> True ornaments to know a holy man.

Richard's professionalism has even thought of the prop. He plays to perfection the part of a holy and retiring man, saddened by the sins of the world, reproving those who encourage ambition for worldly things in him. He maintains the right of the Princes, and when tacitly agreeing to the appeal ('why would you heap this care on me?' 203) suggests an utterly proper sense of the responsibilities kingship entails. (We may be sure that when he says 'I am unfit for state and majesty' the irony is ours, not Richard's, for he has sought nothing else but this.) It is all very clever, and very convincing indeed. Even Richard's delighted and unnecessary rebuke to Buckingham for swearing is a beautiful and entirely credible detail for such a character part.

Richard as actor here reaches his apogee. But his skill has not had the success he hoped, for Buckingham has to do all the talking and keep prodding the Mayor to a response. The support is muted. Richard seems not to be aware of this, and to be delighting more in the quality of his own performance than thinking about its purpose. His successes are not coming as easily as they did. The wooing of the citizens is notably less successful than the wooing of Anne.

His power seems complete in IV.i, but from this point the role-playing

---

* It is perhaps significant that another Vice figure in another political play, Falstaff in *1 Henry IV*, employs the metaphor of acting throughout and has his symbolic values focused for us in a piece of play-acting: see my *Shakespeare's History Plays.*

becomes less assured. Richard's ambition was always for the state of kingship; what he would do as King never crossed his mind, and the reality of the office destroys the pretence of its new holder. He can only fall back, ultimately, on naked tyranny, and the second half of the play shows the once-attractive villain as bloody Senecan tyrant.

With the news of Richard's coronation Elizabeth recognizes the working out of Margaret's curse on her. The Duchess and Anne see something devilish enthroned in power over them. But at the very moment of this success the fragility of Richard's tenure of the high office of kingship, the Vicariate of God on earth, is demonstrated. Firstly, his own security in himself is, we are suddenly told by Anne (IV.i.75–86), cracking: part of Margaret's and Anne's curse is being fulfilled, for he is troubled in his sleep, and that conscience in which he did not believe, yet to which he sanctimoniously appealed in his performance, is becoming a reality he cannot control. Secondly, there is the first hint of the successful countermovement to Richard: Stanley sends Dorset away to join Richmond. Thirdly, when Richard enters in majesty in IV.ii, his first act as King is the act of a tyrant like Herod: to demand of Buckingham the murder of the Princes. He is for the first time feeling his insecurity, and in murdering children he is murdering symbols of that future that he so earnestly planned for and thought within his control. But Buckingham, the man by whose hand he ascends the throne, the one man he trusted, refuses; and he for the first time fails to control his appearance – he cannot hide his agitation, for Catesby notices he 'gnaws his lip' (IV.ii.27).* His confidence in his ability to control response to him suddenly shatters:

> I will converse with iron-witted fools
> And unrespective boys. None are for me
> That look into me with considerate eyes.

> (28–30)

Earlier such 'considerate eyes' watching his performance would not have worried him. And finally, immediately afterwards the news of Dorset's 'flight' is given him, and in addition to the open loss of control over one he treated with contempt there is a loss of psychological self control.

---

* Cf.III.iv.51–3:

> I think there's never a man in Christendom
> Can lesser hide his love or hate than he,
> For by his face straight shall you know his heart.

What was said in jest is proving true.

Richard is having to think on his feet as he has never had to before, for up to this point, as it were, he wrote the script, and now the circumstance, or Fortune, of which he thought he was master, is doing so. The news of Dorset's flight (47ff.) is followed by a revealing ellipsis of thought. Richard calls on Catesby to prepare the ground for Anne dying suddenly: clearly he is seeing his own insecurity and need to strengthen his hold on the crown by marrying the one undoubted heir, Edward's daughter Elizabeth. The lines of soliloquy that follow (59ff.) show a completely new side to Richard. For the first time in the play he is deeply uneasy (62); he is clearly aware for the first time of the enormity of what he proposes (63ff.); and, in a hint of that despair that Macbeth will eventually feel, he tacitly accepts not only the theological concept of sin but also that he is trapped in it by a chain of causality he has himself set in motion. He has lost the one thing he prided himself on and believed to be real* – his freedom to play his own game:

> But I am in
> So far in blood that sin will pluck on sin.

The rhyme stresses the importance of this turning point in Richard; and gone – though not yet for ever – is the old insouciance we associated with his soliloquies before. Furthermore, a little later (94ff.) Richard is clearly not taking much notice of what is going on round him. He is badly rattled, and Buckingham's seeking to attract his attention clearly irritates him further. These lines are almost soliloquy, and in them Richard is for the first time taking prophecy, the prophecy of his own death, seriously. He is afraid.

The downward movement continues. The murderers of Clarence had an access of conscience, and it was at least in some sense comic. Richard's agent Tyrrel has a much more serious access of conscience after arranging the murder of the Princes, and our response to Richard at this point is revulsion – particularly at his lip-smacking satisfaction. In his brief progress report on his plots (36ff.) there is an ironic use of the clichés applicable to death, and even a hint of the old sprezzatura, such as we saw when he accosted Anne, in his picture of himself as a 'jolly thriving wooer' (IV.iii.43) off to win Elizabeth; but it is all said with a sardonic twist that sharply distinguishes it from the early delight in his power to delude. But before he can get started on this project, before his customary momentum can build up, again he is interrupted by bad news: the joining of Ely with Richmond and the revolt of Buckingham.

* Our recognition of him at the start as the Vice, who always is trapped by his own evil even when he thinks himself most free, makes this moment doubly ironic.

The first part of the next scene, IV.iv, has obvious parallels to I.iii, where Richard, in the ascendant of his power, was able to contain and divert the torrent of cursing – and able, too, to divide the opposition to him and set it against itself. Queen Margaret enters, almost like the 'presenter' of a masque (cf. line 5), moralizing and generalizing the play's action. Her first speech echoes lines from the other bereaved characters in the play, and suggests that her curses are growing to a ghastly fruiting. The formal elevated language of the verse and the patterned use of rhyme to link Margaret's acid asides to the sorrow of the Queen and Duchess makes the first moments of the scene seem almost ritual; and when Margaret advances and sits with them the exchanges take on the aspect of a formally patterned litany of guilt and suffering. The guilt in which they all share gradually unites those who earlier were divided in a chorus of abhorrence of Richard. The three, in fact, speak in 1.9–135 a sort of Induction, of lament and execration, to the picture we next get of Richard with his army. When Richard enters he is nonplussed: at first he has no answer to the immediate challenges of his mother and the Queen, takes refuge quite seriously in his role as the Lord's Anointed, the King whose office is holy whatever the failings of the man, and seeks to drown their noise with the roll of drums and noise of trumpets – the visible and audible expression of his power.* He tries to divert his mother from her reproof with frankly rather silly jokes, but her curse – the most terrible of all curses, being a mother's – a foretaste of the curse before the battle of Bosworth, strikes him to silence. In that silence the Queen attempts to redouble the attack in her turn; but Richard can just about cope with her. The situational, conceptual and stylistic parallel with the wooing of Anne is exact: Richard entering where a woman is engaged in ritualized mourning to face a torrent of accusation, of hate, and then, before a silent audience – of mourners, of his army – defending himself with courtesy and outrageous suggestions of his ultimate benevolence and lack of responsibility for the actions he admits, using either extended and plausible argument or rapid stichomythic exchange. There are even echoes of the earlier scene: but 'Say that I did all this for love of her?' (288; which must, I think, be phrased as a question) is far less confident than I.ii.121–4. Richard is taking very hard knocks indeed: whereas in I.ii Anne was fighting on ground of his choosing, here he is fighting on Elizabeth's, and is responding rather than taking the initiative.

---

* The presence of the army, like the presence of the bearers of King Henry's bier, is significant. Both occasions are public; but the presence of an army emphasizes that the verbal wrestling with Elizabeth is literally a battle royal to secure the throne (537–8) and its power. Richard's army shows that though it may be temporary, his power at the moment is real enough.

Elizabeth's attack is very powerful: he gets better than he gives in the stichomythia of 342ff. The antiphonal lines ram together conflicting ideas, and each idea he proposes is shattered by her. Elizabeth turns his own words back against him by altering their pattern to reverse the sense; for the first time he is being beaten at his own argumentative and linguistic game. She sees his mastery of language as essentially meretricious; his oaths are worthless since he has devalued or stolen the things he swears by; his actions have separated him from his self, the world, his honourable descent, his God (374ff.). There is a sense of Richard's being fought closer and closer to the wall in this exchange, of his growing and irrevocable isolation. He is forced in the end, by swearing by 'The time to come' (387), to acknowledge his guilt and worthlessness; yet in killing the children, Richard has killed the time to come. The future he always took for granted, to which he always worked, is running out for him. We, the audience, know that Bosworth is only a short while away. Even the promise of repentance, a last throw of the sanctimony that was so useful, is relegated to that unachievable future (398). And in the end, when Elizabeth has shown that all other realities by which a man can swear have no meaning for him, he is forced to prove to her the love and goodwill he pretends by cursing himself: an insincere curse that is fulfilled in detail. The self destroys the self (399ff.). Elizabeth is still unrelenting; she sees him as a devil tempting her, and her final replies to him are questions that recall his guilt.

Nevertheless it seems as if, against all the odds, he is going to pull this one off too, and clearly Richard's contemptuous explosion, 'Relenting fool, and shallow-changing woman!' when Elizabeth leaves (431) shows that he thinks he has done. But Elizabeth does not agree to what he demands; we are left in real doubt as to the outcome. His overconfidence in his cleverness makes him think she has agreed, but no such construction can logically be put on her words. She has won time. The actor has been taken in by his own skill, and what is most surprising is that he had such a hard fight from one whom in the beginning of the play he hardly bothered about as a menace.

The apparent success is again undercut by a hurly burly of mainly bad news (433ff.). Richmond's arrival throws Richard into something very like panic. His energy attempts to send people off in all directions, but he forgets to tell them what to do. When Stanley enters, it is quite clear that he is afraid of Richard's anger, and that Richard is no longer bothering to make any pretence of just monarchy: the tyrant shows himself for what he is by demanding Stanley's son as hostage. But Richard has not enough fingers to plug the leaky dyke; more messengers with more bad news, and

Richard is so rattled he so far forgets what belongs to a King to strike the man – ironically, the one who brings news that Buckingham is no longer a menace. None of this very fast, even confused, action, is in Richard's control: like Macbeth, who was also able to win a crown by self-conscious and self-controlled deceit, Richard now is merely at the mercy of events, responding to the reaction his rise to the throne has called up.

The last act of Richard's performance is at Bosworth. Again Shakespeare deploys the techniques of the Morality: the two tents, of Richard and Richmond, side by side on stage, the two combatants point for point – almost allegorically – compared, the one confiding himself to heaven and blessed by dreams of comfort, the other reduced to a reliance on a self that no longer exists coherently, damned by nightmares of the victims he has brought to bloody end. The pattern is exactly exploited, even to ritual combat between Good and Evil; for Shakespeare is interested in exploring the contrast not just between a good King and a bad one – which would hardly be worth doing – but, in these closing moments, looking at the essential negativeness of evil. Gone is the witty self-possession and awareness of distance of Richard's early scenes, and he is now a character on the same level as everyone else: his first words on the field are a nervous inquiry about the time followed by worry about his armour (V.iii.47ff.: one is reminded of Macbeth's impatience for the fight and irritation with his armour, V.iii.30ff.). His fluent and supple speech has degenerated into short sentences governed by verbs in the imperative or interrogative mood. His sleep is full of nightmares of wounding and battle.

It was conventional for tyrants, of Senecan or other descent, to have bad sleep. Richard, as we have seen, is just such a tyrant when he becomes King, and his dream is not in itself that unusual. There is also a long tradition that allowed the tragic hero in his final moments a self-questioning that allowed him to perceive a shape to his progress. But Shakespeare has given Richard a speech of more than usual point and complexity. For one thing, it balances that other dream of guilt and terror at the other end of the play, Clarence's (see pp. 38–9), and the two together analyse the landscape of the mind in Hell and the guilt that leads to that horror. Richard begins to take himself apart as if he were another person in a seesaw of self-accusation and self-excuse, and he divides the self he has taken for granted into two Richards, one who can no longer escape the realization of a moral law the other has flouted and in so doing destroyed his integrity. Both selves, and therefore both voices in the speech, are mutually antagonistic. The short sharp jerky questions balanced by short sharp replies recall the stichomythic exchanges with his adversaries in I.ii and IV.iv, but now it is Richard who is adversary to himself. The mind which has been in total control from the first soliloquy now breaks into two warring halves – both of them 'Fool' (193). The one half has achieved that selfish fulfilment designed from the first soliloquy, and does not know what to do with it; the other half is dominated by a consciousness of that sin Richard momentarily glimpsed, and is full of self-hatred. And both halves are Richard. The integrity, the self-reliance and self-control of the Machiavellian 'new man', who denied the validity or reality of the moral order, is here seen to be a sham, even though it gave him his initial power over others less single-minded than himself. The consciousness of guilt, and despair in the face of it, reduces a man who filled the world to a desire for nothingness. And the irony in so articulating this profound discovery is that Richard can no longer act, not even to himself. There is not even any escape into the illusory truth of metaphor, for the speech is devoid of them. The very rhetoric of the speech echoes the division of the self: antithesis and parallelism, isocolon, epistrophe, anadiplosis – all the figures stress the notion of division and ambiguity. Indeed, just as Richard used his body as a prop to establish himself in the first speech of the play, here through the nature of the expression of the thought the mind is being used as a prop to indicate the nothingness at the heart of the evil man.

He now knows real fear (215), and even descends to the indignity of eavesdropping. But despite the sickness at the heart, when the occasion comes he can put on a good act as a warlike and decisive monarch. One of the paradoxes of the play is that monster as Richard is at the end there is an upward movement that wins for him a good deal of sympathy and leaves us with a perceptible sense of loss. There is a desperate and not unadmirable courage in his pushing away the idea of conscience (see p. 83) that has just so racked him in the short speech of semi-soliloquy at 309ff., a certain magnificence in his acceptance of Hell. The oration to his soldiers is the last time he plays the orator. It is a good example of the genre; it shows the old command of the appropriate rhetorical register, the mastery of tone and the sense of an audience and how to woo them that marked Richard in his earlier days. And all that then remains to him is to play the act to the end: to meet his opposite. And he does so with a magnificent final burst of energy and courage. Richmond, ingloriously if sensibly, had several men disguised as himself, whom Richard has killed; and Richard 'enacts . . . wonders', goes down fighting, seeking for Richmond in the throat of that death whose minister he has himself been. His play is over.

*

Acting a part, then, *is* Richard's truth. But there is one part no man, not even he, can act or simulate: that of King. That role demands, as Henry V is made to realize, whole and total commitment. The discussion above (p. 7ff) of degree and *ordo* has indicated some of the ideas attaching to kingship in Renaissance thought. Fundamental is the notion of the King's Two Bodies, the one fallible, human and temporary, the other holy, immortal, the deputy of God and fount of law and justice which speaks through him.* Long after the idea had ceased to have the serious force it did in the Renaissance Coleridge expressed the heart of it beautifully:

I respect the man while, and only while, the king is translucent through him: I reverence the glass case for the Saint's sake within; except for that, it is to me mere glazier's work, – putty, and glass, and wood.

(*Table Talk*, 20 August 1830)

In the use of the royal 'we' something of this concept survives: the plural denoted that through the mouth of a single man the will of the King and people acting in concert is expressed. The mortal man, fallible and temporary, has to subordinate himself to the demands of the immortal role of God's Vicar on earth and be subsumed into its mystical reality and the part therefore cannot be simulated. Richard's usurpation of the role, which his ironic definition of it as a 'world of cares' (III.vii.222) shows (because he *is* ironic) he understands it not a whit, and means that he is necessarily judged by it. What is said to deceive the Mayor we recognize as truth:

> I am unfit for state and majesty . . .
> For God doth know, and you may partly see,
> How far I am from the desire of this.

(III.vii,204,234–5)

He does not know what to do with the kingship he has aimed at single-mindedly except try to strengthen his own position; he is unable even to glimpse an idea of himself as fulfilling a role as God's scourge, as – with undeniable overconfidence – Marlowe's Tamburlaine the Great does. The separate commands of the injunction in I Peter 2:17, so often quoted in Elizabethan pulpits, 'Love the brotherhood. Fear God. Honour the King,' usually, in a normal polity, are convergent; but in Richard's state brothers are murdered, as Cain murdered Abel, to fear God is to hate

* See my *Shakespeare's History Plays*. The conception is an extension to extreme form of the Renaissance understanding of the relationship between individual character and public role – see above, p. 43f.

everything the King stands for, and to honour the King is to ignore the claims of divine law.

The true King is a reconciler, one who through justice and mercy harmonizes the polity of men with the polity of the heavens. Even Edward, with all his faults as King, had tried to be a reconciler, on his deathbed seeking to persuade enemies – who are members of the same house and family – to overcome their hatred with love:

> And more in peace my soul shall part to heaven,
> Since I have made my friends at peace on earth . . .
> Dissemble not your hatred, swear your love.

> (II.i.5ff.)

Richmond, the saviour of the whole tetralogy, is given a choric statement of the family restored:

> We will unite the White Rose and the Red.
> Smile, heaven, upon this fair conjunction,
> That long have frowned upon their enmity . . .
> O, now let Richmond and Elizabeth,
> The true succeeders of each royal house,
> By God's fair ordinance conjoin together!
> And let their heirs, God, if Thy will be so,
> Enrich the time to come with smooth-faced peace,
> With smiling plenty, and fair prosperous days!

> (V.v.19–21, 29ff.)

The opposite to the true King is the tyrant, for whom power and its exercise is merely selfish. Richard as King demonstrates in his tyranny the true nature of Machiavellian ambition and ignoring of the moral law, and as we have seen it is when he became King that he ceases to personate; he shows what he personally is. For Richard is above all a divider of men from each other: he divides Clarence from his brother's affection, Anne from the body of the King she mourns and who represents for her all she valued, Catesby from his patron Hastings – an important touch, given the reliance of sixteenth-century politics on the relationship between patrons and clients; he is a divider of the family, a divider, ultimately, of his own self into nothingness. Richard's acting brings him to the point where he can no longer act in any sense: the division between what he truly is and what he pretends to be, which he thinks he can use as a mere tool in a game to achieve his ends, becomes finally no game at all: he finds he has two mutually antagonistic selves, with mutually exclusive values.

7. Conscience and the King – Some Themes of the Play

The actor has no conscience in his role: the man who plays Iago does not lie sleepless on his bed for guilt at what he does. But Richard the actor discovers that what was play is all too real, and that conscience, the worm that dieth not, torments him with guilt. The moment of this recognition does not suddenly happen, though it is sudden enough in Richard. It has been prepared for throughout the play, and indeed it is perfectly possible (though I think mistaken) to play Richard as a man whose implicit rejection of conscience by his delight in his own clever villainy betokens a conscience of real force. Conscience is important enough in the play to be called one of its themes, and it relates to the issue raised earlier about the vulnerability of the ordered system of the world to the man who rejects its values (p. 53f), the Machiavellian. In the end the Machiavellian who thinks himself free of moral restraint is defeated by the moral order of the universe contained in little, micro-cosmically, in his own self.

The discussion of conscience is concentrated in the figures of Clarence, his murderers, Buckingham and Tyrrel. Clarence shows no hint of conscience in I.i when he is on his way to the Tower, but a night there, like Richard's night before Bosworth (cf. above, p. 75f), changes him radically. Like Richard, he has nightmares:

> ... as I am a Christian faithful man,
> I would not spend another such a night
> Though 'twere to buy a world of happy days.

(I.iv.4ff.)

But he is not a faithful man: he is 'false, fleeting, perjured Clarence', and repentance and its attendant suffering are the only ways to purchase the happiness of salvation. Clarence's own terms indicate his moral confusion, and later (50ff.) the operation of his own mind forces him to recognize his sins – breaking of faith, murder. The dream he describes to the Keeper I have discussed above, p. 38f, and recognition of its type shows the Hell that Clarence, if unrepentant, is doomed to. By I.iv.66ff. he accepts the moral truth of his dream, confesses his crimes, 'For Edward's sake', and acknowledges his standing under God's judgement (69ff.). This is to be taken entirely seriously; and Clarence is not un-attractive in his hope that God's mercy will stop his sins being visited on

79

his wife and children. (Yet the experience of history shows that the innocent suffer for the guilty.) Already the power of the language in the dream has made us take Clarence much more seriously than his first appearance in the play might have suggested we should. Right at the beginning we saw him, almost with conspiratorial approval, as a victim (I.i.32ff.) whose potential suffering was washed away in the force of Richard's attractiveness. Now we are seeing him on his own as a man suffering realization of what he is, not just something to be manipulated, and Richard's humour is not there to mask the reality. Clarence's pathos and access of moral understanding throw a very bad light indeed on Richard.

Clarence's pleading with the murderers and urging of the claims on them of divine law exacerbate the doubts that the Second Murderer already entertains about their enterprise. It is unnecessary to go through the argument with them in detail; Clarence grows in moral authority and dignity as well as pathos in the course of it, and the indignity of his end, stabbed in the back and then dragged off to be drowned in the malmsey-butt (anticipated earlier, I.iv.157, 165), does nothing to destroy this.* The murderers themselves take a stage further the play's discussion of the reality of conscience and the innate moral law it betokens.

The two murderers restate in a comic mode the access of conscience Clarence has felt. The switch to prose at I.iv.83 indicates a drop in tone, decorous to the station of the murderers, and also a drop in apparent seriousness. Their language has all the verbal agility Shakespeare's later clowns show, and their first exchange when left by Brackenbury is obviously to be played for a laugh (99–102) about something which is in fact deadly serious. Already the Second Murderer's question and the First's reply have sketched in their differing characters – the Second Murderer is much more apologetic and unsure than the First, who is the man of action priding himself on his directness and freedom from scruple. Almost immediately the Second Murderer has an access of remorse, and comically mentions the motif, judgement, that Clarence is to urge to them both much more powerfully later. But the Second Murderer soon is reassured by the thought of reward, and rejects the idea of conscience on utilitarian – Machiavellian! – grounds in a speech that looks straight forward to Falstaff's reduction of another abstract idea forceful in men's lives, honour, to mere 'air' on the field of Shrewsbury (128ff.). Ironically, the speech that the Second Murderer uses to persuade himself to work

---

* The incident is comic precisely because it is in such bad taste, so humiliating; our laughter is a relief from the horror. It also relates through the imagery to the idea of Richard devouring his victims – see p. 107.

unsettles the resolve of the first (148), and the Second Murderer urges him, in the very tones of a concerned parson, to 'Take [i.e. arrest] the devil in thy mind – and believe him not' – equating the prompting of conscience with the temptations of Satan! It is now the Second Murderer who wants to 'fall to work', but it is still the first who has the ideas (156ff.).

When Clarence wakes, the lift to verse indicates rising tension and seriousness. The First Murderer does most of the talking. But when Clarence warns them of the vengeance of God, the Second Murderer speaks with a new authority, challenging Clarence with the crimes he has committed; the first uses a deliberately revolting image to remind Clarence of his murder of his sovereign's son. The two silence him momentarily with their accusations, and the first murderer's lines –

> How canst thou urge God's dreadful law to us
> When thou hast broke it in such dear degree?

– suggest that Clarence's crimes are so bad that their murdering of him hardly comes within the scope of God's dreadful law – they are administering justice. Their very language (209ff., for example) acquires an authority of rhythm and an elevation of expression that suggests the seriousness of what they are saying, and the First Murderer's turning back on him of Clarence's syntactical and linguistic pattern (212) momentarily reminds us of the accusatory mode of Anne's challenge to Richard. The crosscurrents in this part of the scene are pretty complex, and in the Second Murderer's relative silence between 222 and 252 one can sense some sort of struggle. Certainly 'Make peace with God, for you must die, my lord' (252), with its curious mixture of 'God' with the murder to be committed by the speaker and the respectful 'my lord', suggests that the word 'must' implies both that Clarence deserves death, with the Second Murderer seeing himself like an executioner, and a hesitation in his resolve. Clarence's final appeal to them, that they are not executioners but will be as guilty as they maintain him to be if they kill him, does strike home; and the Second Murderer seems to have decided against the act when he warns Clarence in 271. After the killing, the Second Murderer's dominant feeling is remorse, while the first thinks only of practicalities.

The scene already shows that mastery of the technique of differentiation and individuation of minor characters that is so noticeable in Shakespeare's mature drama. But it is far more than just a blackly comic interlude. Clarence's death and what has led up to it is not funny, for Clarence has engaged our sympathy. Hence our attitude to the murderers is at best ambivalent. But when we recall that the real murderer is Richard, and that these are merely his tools, the significance of the scene becomes clearer. These two murderers share a good deal of the downbeat cynical humour of Richard himself; the First Murderer's idea to drown Clarence in a butt of wine echoes Richard's ironic remark to Clarence in I.i.49f: 'belike his majesty hath some intent That you should be new-christened in the Tower.' The Second Murderer's rejection of conscience (I.iv.128ff.) transposes into a lower register the attitude and tone of Richard's cynical first soliloquy. It echoes the idea of personal advantage as a determinant of moral attitude; and, like that first soliloquy, it is spoken as much to display in a self-reassuring way wit and invention as to argue a point. The mock morality of 139ff. anticipates the sanctimony of Richard. The altercation with Clarence, turning round ideas of justice and deserts, echoes the nub of the confrontation with Anne. The echoes seem to be deliberate, and the conclusion suggests itself that in the two we are seeing Richard externalized with his winning humour and self-confidence removed. And when we watch the ebb and flow of conscience in the two men, and the final separation of them into one who feels remorse and guilt and one who does not, it is difficult to escape the conclusion that Shakespeare is using this scene almost allegorically, to represent a psychomachia that does in fact take place in Richard's own mind before Bosworth, to indicate the psychological division into non-sense that the evil man inevitably undergoes. There he who had been utterly single of purpose is divided into two warring halves, the one overwhelmed with conscience and remorse, the other holding fast like the First Murderer to practicality and dismissing those ideas that cannot be quantified, analysed and measured. The crown can be held in the hand; so can 'meed'. We have already seen that the play is using a good many techniques and presupposes a lot of the expectations of the old Morality drama, and the use of the two murderers makes very good sense if we explore it on these lines. Doing so warns us that the reality – or not – of conscience and what it stands for is a major issue in the play.

Approaching the scene of the dreams before Bosworth as allegorical in conception is also fruitful. The polar moral opposition between Richmond and Richard is visibly expressed by having their tents on either side of the stage. The ghosts, victims all of Richard's crimes, speak stilted, formally patterned verse to each in turn, blessing Richmond and acting to Richard exactly as the murderers do to Clarence, challenging him to recall and recognize his crimes. The scene is like nothing so much as a morality play; the ghosts make explicit in a visual and outward sign the inner reality and state of the two opponents: they are Richard's bad conscience and Richmond's good one, and spur him on as agent of justice. The result of these apparitions, this externalization of what is internal, is Richard's agonized perception of the nonentity, the incoherence of the self he worshipped and whose behaviour he so admired. The detachment from himself, the ability to applaud himself as an actor in a role free of all moral restraints, has brought him to the point of really seeing what he is and not what he thinks he is.

Yet Richard denies the reality of the very idea of conscience – he could not play with it as he does if he took it seriously, for he would be knowingly self-contradictory and self-damning: part at least of the comedy of the play is that Richard does not see how the rug is always ready to be pulled from under him. When he says at III.vii.222ff. to the Mayor and citizens,

> Will you enforce me to a world of cares?
> Call them again. I am not made of stone,
> But penetrable to your kind entreaties,
> Albeit against my conscience and my soul,

he cannot take seriously either the conscience he expects them to believe in or the existence of his own soul. When he has already begun to see just how wrong he is, in one of those moments of semi-soliloquy that occur with increasing frequency towards the end, he turns aside from his suite to try to encourage himself by asserting what he always took for granted – by whistling in the dark:

> Let not our babbling dreams affright our souls;
> Conscience is but a word that cowards use,
> Devised at first to keep the strong in awe.
> Our strong arms be our conscience, swords our law!

(V.iii.309)

All the evidence is against him now. Conscience is a not just a *word*, not just a fiction invented as a political tool; force is useless against it. It is real, and it destroys. In those lines the central issue of Richard's view of existence is laid bare: that values are mere words, mere conventions, that the brave man can overcome if he have will enough. To that issue we shall return later, for it is integral to the language and philosophy of the play (see p. 108f).

The balancing of Clarence's dream and Richard's, of the murderers' dialogue against Richard's soliloquy, is thus strategic to Shakespeare's analysis of the reality and force of conscience. The issue is further highlighted, and its connection with providential justice suggested, in the development of minor characters.

Clarence's guiltiness must in some way be extenuated by his loyalty to his brother and his selfless service of Edward's interests (cf. I.iv.214). His crimes are not thereby excused, any more than the murderers' are by being agents of Richard; nevertheless, the motivation is not dishonourable in itself, though the means to the end are appalling. Just as, therefore, Richard takes much responsibility for the murderers, so Edward must for Clarence. In II.i., where Edward is trying to be a reconciler, to put a period to the strife he knows is just beneath the surface, the picture of Clarence he gives in 106ff. is highly attractive. Clarence was noble, generous, encouraging to him, and Edward's sorrow and shock at the news of his death sound genuine. That news, however, is more than an excuse to increase the pathos of Clarence's murder. It cuts the ground completely from under Edward's attempt at reconciliation, and the dying King from that point on is locked into realizing how little real accord is possible in a society dominated by factional jealousy (107ff., 120–31) and a remembrance of the strife and crime that brought him to the throne. In the end he fears the justice of God, recognizing that he is to blame both as King and as a man for the suffering he sees as inescapable. He recognizes that the man who is guilty himself can never be the reconciler the kingdom needs, and the entail of suffering goes on.

As that suffering comes, as Margaret's curse is exactly fulfilled, all Richard's victims come to recognize that whatever the hateful author of their suffering, they are getting only what they deserve: that their past which they thought behind them is rising up to challenge their present. The pattern of exact justice is not only of interest in itself, but also for the way it forces each sinner at the moment of crisis or death to a self-evaluation and acceptance of guilt. That means virtually everyone in the play, and the long perspective of crime and rebellion in the *Henry VI* plays and ultimately, in history, reaching back to the deposition of Richard II by Bolingbroke, is purged in these men and women. The universality in the play of a sense of guilt suggests that it is not just individuals, but England itself that has self-knowingly to expiate its crime of disobedience to its natural lord.

Tyrrel, 'Whose humble means match not his haughty spirit' (IV.ii.37), suffers on a lower social level from precisely that ambition and avarice that has motivated the chief actors in this national disobedience. He appears virtually from nowhere: the page's casual knowledge of him (IV.ii.36ff.) suggests that in Edward's and Richard's kingdom murderers are on tap.* He arranges without a qualm the murder of the innocent Princes, the hopes of the future, through intermediaries. But as soon as the murders are done, even the 'fleshed villains, bloody dogs' (IV.iii.6) were overcome with remorse and conscience. Tyrrel's lingering quotation of Dighton and Forrest's description of the children (which is pathetically pretty, to the point of being cloying) indicates that he as well as they has been overcome by conscience and consciousness of what the crime means. Dighton and Forrest's semantics suggest a dim awareness that they have not only killed children, but the possibility of growth and fruitfulness – the 'summer beauty' of the 'four red roses on a stalk' † will now never fruit, and Nature's last best work is ruined (17–18). Richard is now 'the bloody King' (22); this moment marks a turning away from him because of innate moral self-recognition of even those who are his natural supporters and tools. His isolation is progressively increased, as even his natural counsellor and confidant, Buckingham, jibs at the course of action he wants (IV.iii).

Buckingham is an important figure in the play, especially because he does not seem to feel the access of conscience in quite the same way as other characters. Since his career was a matter of common knowledge before the play began, his early appearances, when he seems a decent enough nobleman, must be seen as consummate dissembling of his own motivation. In an important sense therefore he is a foil to Richard, another Machiavellian politician who makes power his chief good and does not consider the morality of how he gets it. Liberated from conscience and the moral law, for him politics are purely politics, an area where morality is irrelevant.

In I.iii, his is the last voice to join in the chorus of vilification of Margaret (I.iii.186), and he tries to quieten her by appealing to charity or shame (272; 284). This elicits from her (279ff.) a warning about trusting Richard too far; as we have not yet seen him linked with Richard this is a useful bit of 'backward plotting'. But he scorns Margaret:

---

* It is thus attractive to see him as one of those 'representative' figures in the play, like the Scrivener and the Mayor (see above, pp. 69–70). That Shakespeare was in fact working on this sort of line is supported by the figure of Brackenbury, who is historically not associated with Clarence's death at all, since he was not appointed Lieutenant of the Tower till 1483. But his presence in I.i and I.iv links Clarence's murder, Richard's first act in the play, with his last, that of the Princes, who were killed while he was, as everybody knew, in charge of the Tower (cf. IV.i.15ff.). He is also a useful mouthpiece for the little homily on the fragility and illusion of the power for which Clarence, Edward, Richard and others strive (I.iv.76–83).

† The impossibility of visualizing the children in this vegetable way suggests that the ideas are to be taken emblematically, symbolically, rather than merely as description.

the present reality of Richard, and his possible usefulness, is more powerful with him than the 'sin, death, and hell' Margaret sees marking Richard. Because he 'soothes the devil', Margaret prophesies his fall.

This visible choice of Richard's patronage rather than Margaret's warning prepares for the rapid development between the two men of the nearest thing Richard shows to intimacy in the whole play. In II.ii Buckingham enters not alone or with other lords, as before, but with Richard. His apparent good faith is suddenly undercut at the end of the scene by remaining behind with Richard to plot the detachment of the Queen's kindred from the Prince, and Richard now calls him

> My other self, my counsel's consistory,
> My oracle, by prophet, my dear cousin.

(II.ii.151f.)

The likeness between them is very strongly stressed, and throwing the vow of reconciliation of II.i to the winds, by II.iv.45ff. he is acting against the Woodvilles with Richard.

From this point Buckingham is more and more important as Richard's henchman, feed and foil. In III.i.44ff. he argues down the old Cardinal's instinctive and honourable feeling against removing the Princes from their mother in sanctuary courteously, with convincing rationality, on the grounds of present necessity. This encounter, brief as it is, is symbolic at all points: the young man representative of a new age versus the old, the man of politics against the churchman, intellect and analysis against faith and an instinct of what is holy. Yet Buckingham seems well enough disposed towards the Princes, if not to their mother (152). He is playing his own game against the Queen's party, and is using Richard as Richard is using him.

The association with Richard reaches its climax in III.v and III.vii (see above, p. 69f). Buckingham plays his role as supporter, co-plotter, manipulator, co-actor and cheerleader for Richard with gusto. His public speeches to win support appeal to the national good, and to all the approved values which it is impossible for him to hold. His main concern is simply power. In IV.i it is his hand that helps Richard to the throne, and in that scene he expects his reward from a Richard he is naive enough to expect him to be grateful. But the logical conclusion of the course of action he has followed so far is to cooperate in the murder of the Princes, which he refuses to do. The Machiavellian politician has to go the whole hog if he is to be safe, and Buckingham fails to realize this. Recognizing his danger, he is quite ready to turn against Richard for his own safety and enter into alliance with Richmond, but Margaret's and his own curse catch up with him. In V.i he recognizes the justice of what has happened to him, that his 'feignèd prayer' has been fulfilled by the 'All-seer which I dallied with' (V.i.20), that he has been 'punish[ed] with hate in those where I expect most love' (II.i.34–5).

But at the very end there is no agony of mind, as for example there is in Clarence. Buckingham gets no further than a grim perception of patterns, that the rules of the game were different to what he supposed, and that he has lost it. There is a certain sardonic dignity in him as he is led off to execution, and his death has none of the pathos of Clarence's or the recognition of their own complicity in crime of Grey, Rivers and Vaughan (III.iii.15f.). Buckingham is a man who is spiritually dead.

Justice, Vengeance, Revenge

A play where nearly every character is forced to recognize the bearing of the past crime on his own present cannot avoid being in some sense a discussion of causality in human affairs and of the shape of history. Commonly in Elizabethan thought the reign of Richard III was seen as demonstrating in a peculiarly neat way the operation of Providence and God's justice. Sir Walter Ralegh, for example, in his *History of the World* (1614) * says of the reign of Edward IV, 'this *Edward* the King . . . beheld and allowed the slaughter which *Gloucester*, *Dorset*, *Hastings*, and others, made of *Edward* the Prince in his own presence; of which tragical Actors, there was not one that escaped the Judgement of GOD in the same kind' (Sig. B2V). He could quite as easily be referring to Shakespeare's play as to his own historical sources. Queen Margaret in IV.iv sees in the sufferings of her enemies the action of an 'upright, just, and true-disposing God' (55) who is presiding over the events. But the issue of Providence is not as simple as either Ralegh or Queen Margaret (who is, after all, a fictional character circumscribed by the demands of the fiction in which she appears) make it sound.

Francis Bacon in several places has some shrewd things to say about poetry and drama and its relationship to life. In *The Advancement of Learning* (1605), II.iv.2, he echoes Aristotle and his Renaissance commentators with a certain reserve: poetry is

nothing else but feigned history . . . The use of this feigned history hath been to give some shadow of satisfaction to the mind of man in those points wherein the nature of things doth deny it . . . Because true history propoundeth the successes and issues of actions not so agreeable to the merits of virtue and vice, therefore poesy feigns them more just in retribution, and more according to revealed providence.

* By the time he wrote it his attitude looked a little old-fashioned.

Bacon is much more representative than Ralegh of the more sceptical temper of the turn of the century; he knew his Machiavelli, he knew his history, and he was deeply interested in how the coherence of a fiction, be it made as a philosophical system or the powerful experience of poetry, can affect men so that they perceive reality not as it is but as they expect or wish it to be. I find it difficult to avoid seeing this issue in *Richard III*; it is moreover an issue closely related to the philosophical question of the meaningfulness of general abstract concepts in our language – a problem to which I shall return.

We have already seen that *Richard III* is a made fiction, deliberately shaped from the sources available to Shakespeare to do a particular job. Thus immediately it comes within the scope of Bacon's challenge, and what we have to determine is what Shakespeare is doing with his fiction.*
The heavy patterning of the play certainly seems to indicate a concern to express a neatness and exact balance in the relationship between crime and punishment, but in a play so full of irony at every level, including the irony of our double response to Richard, we perhaps need to be wary.

There is one quite obvious reading of the issue of Providence and Justice in the play which we can take as a baseline. It was known Richard failed; thus all his bustling activity is comic, for Time and Providence have the laugh on him. It was also known that with his death at Bosworth the long period of civil war that began when Henry IV deposed Richard II was brought to a stop with the virtual annihilation of the warring families. The writing of the *Henry VI* and *Richard III* plays does explicitly draw attention to the way present events mesh with those of the past, and there is in the tetralogy a pattern of exact retaliatory vengeance. Crime plucks on retributory crime, and the sinner who punishes the sinner is acting, wittingly or not, as the agent of a God who – as Buckingham explicitly recognizes – is not mocked. 'Vengeance is mine, I will repay, saith the Lord' – the base text of the revenge tragedy genre is never very far from the surface, especially in *Richard III*. It is a consummate irony that Richard, the man who punishes, who executes the will of Providence, is not punishing *for* past crime, but to advance his own future, and moves through the world of the play being recognized as the unwitting agent of a Providence he does not believe in. As he does so, he heaps all the crimes of the English onto his own head, and with his

---

* It might also be of interest to question how audience response to the play might project onto it what is expected of it from its subject – but our evidence for contemporary detailed philosophical response is slight, and the question therefore cannot properly be handled.

final destruction the world is purged. In a sense he could never understand, he is a scourge of Heaven to cleanse and purify; power is allotted
to him for a season for just that purpose. In his nature and his ugliness
he is an epitome of all the wrongs done to this noble realm of England, a
summation of the world others have made in his cruel ambition, his
hypocrisy, his godless faith in the unlimited powers of his own will. His
reign, indeed, can be seen as the penalty England must pay for her
original rejection of Richard II.

But I do not think Shakespeare left it there. The neat fiction is just a
bit too neat not to be disquieting. The figure of Margaret (see p. 91f) is
scarcely attractive, despite the majesty of her presence or the authority
of her language. She is steeped in crime herself. She is positively gleeful
at seeing others suffer what she has suffered: in her, suffering has reduced
the capacity for the noble emotions of compassion and pity. All she is
really interested in is not justice but the personal satisfaction of seeing
others not get away with it, of enjoying a mother's suffering for the
death of an innocent child irrespective of the enormity of the child's
death. This is an absolute travesty of the justice of God which, as the
Bible makes quite clear, is always tempered by mercy. There is no shred
of mercy anywhere in this play. Margaret's literalist interpretation of the
promise of God in Exodus 20:5–6 to 'visit the iniquity of the fathers
upon the children unto the third and fourth generation' omits to reckon
with the continuation of the text: '. . . of them that hate me. And shewing
mercy unto thousands of them that love me'; her understanding of justice
is an endless and unendable exchange of eyes and teeth. And there were
pulpits in Shakespeare's own day, and not a few of them, from which
just such odious sentiments were being preached.

There is no mercy in the play. But it could be argued that in emphasizing the issue of justice and vengeance so much, Shakespeare is drawing
attention to the mercy of Providence operating in the most unexpected
quarter imaginable: in the person of Richard. If he is in fact a symptom
of the realm's disease, his usurpation a symbol of its collective madness,
where Will has usurped the seat of Reason, then his heaping on himself
of all the crimes of the past, subsuming them all and cleaning up the
mess of a century, is a signal act of God's mercy. For when Richard is
gone, the world is cleansed. Even his power to do evil may hint at that
mercy: though it is true that the innocent Princes are destroyed in that
power, its exercise does allow the other criminals to realize what they
are, and perhaps to start – as Clarence surely does – on the road to
repentance that may help them to escape the pains of Hell.

So when characters in the play talk of providence or justice or punishment or vengeance, we need to recognize that they are surrounded by an irony they cannot perceive. Their concepts are shown to be only limitedly and not absolutely true by the frame we perceive round them, and it must therefore follow that the deeper understanding we are able to arrive at may itself be only provisional. The pattern of Providence and justice we see is not that which, say, Margaret sees; but unless we argue a priori – which we can if we want – we cannot say that our own is necessarily more right. Just when we feel most confident about it, at the end of the play, Shakespeare plays two awkward tricks on us: we suddenly cannot avoid feeling *regret* at Richard's death (see p. 76) and a corresponding impatience with the worthy and soothing dullness of Richmond. The bad King is far more exciting than the one we are taught to believe was a good one. And as soon as we think about Richmond, we remember that nowhere in the play is there any shred of a hint that he has any right to the throne except by force of arms – by charging in when all is nearly lost, like the US Cavalry in a Western, and killing the Senecan tyrant who is his rival.* But if Providence operates through hierarchy, degree, lineal succession, and so on, this is distinctly odd: the replacement of one usurper by another. A dynastic marriage and mere aristocratic endorsement of the *fait accompli* does not remove this difficulty: in fact it intensifies it. In some way, therefore, the play must be examining the relationship of the problematical concepts of justice, providence and vengeance to the hierarchical and moral model of the world on which those concepts seem to depend and which they seem to express.

Time and the Importance of Margaret

The issue of a purposive Providence executing justice cannot in this play at least be separated from the notion of time. Richard and Margaret more than any other characters are made to concern themselves with time: they divide it between them. Richard's interest is all in 'the time to come'; Margaret is quite unhistorically introduced into the play to embody the wrong done in past time operating in the present. Regarded strictly as a character, she is pretty lifeless, without depth or development.

---

* Richard is made to draw attention to the *illegitimacy* of Richmond's challenge to his own illegitimate rule in IV.iv.469:

> Is the chair empty? Is the sword unswayed?
> Is the King dead? The empire unpossessed?
> What heir of York is there alive but we?
> And who is England's king but great York's heir?

But as the memory of a suffering England, guilty herself, she has a kind of rock-like integrity as a mouthpiece of an approaching Nemesis whom nobody takes seriously until disaster actually strikes them.

Margaret's function in the formal economy of the play is quite clear: Shakespeare has used her to do the job he found the Chorus doing in Seneca's plays. The Chorus was often distinct from the action, observing and commenting on it from a position of greater knowledge and memory, drawing attention to the implications of action and suggesting a response to it. But the unnamed Chorus has severe limitations, and Shakespeare and his contemporaries sought to overcome the danger of excessive distancing and dramatic stiffness by giving the Chorus function to characters who could be involved as required in the action of the drama. At the same time they retained the important choric function of framing or valuing the action, so that its significance could be drawn out.

The Spanish Tragedy, for example, opens with a 'framing' prologue (I.i) between the Ghost of Andrea and the personification of Revenge. At the very simplest level this is useful for exposition, to supply necessary background to the subsequent action. But it also is used to underline the areas of interest in that action, and to suggest a theme. Within the play proper, Kyd is very ready to use, for example in II.ii, two characters, Lorenzo and Balthasar, visible to the audience and not to Horatio and Belimperia, to comment on the love scene between them. We have seen already that Shakespeare uses Richard as Chorus/Prologue to his own tragedy (I.i), stressing the nature of his actions in the future time we shall watch in the play. Margaret first appears in I.iii.108 as an eavesdropper like Lorenzo and Balthasar, providing a detailed commentary on the past of every character who speaks. This is a fine piece of theatre: the foreground filled with the wrangling figures, whose quarrels after 110 are thrown into a belittling perspective by Margaret's insistent recalling of their crimes. Her remarks bubble with bitterness and hate; her recollection of the past teaches her to curse. In a sense she is the past personified, for she has been at the heart of political events in the previous reign. She is herself a cruel and wicked woman, who will delight in seeing others suffer as she has done. Nevertheless, when she comes forward her enormous authority, both in the momentum of her rhetoric and in what she is as a living history of England, dominates the stage completely. The insistent recital of past crime strips bare the real nature of this court. In her curses, Margaret looks to a future when all will be punished: it is not the real purpose of suffering – recognition of one's fault and reformation – to which she looks forward, but just to the cruel joy of seeing her enemies suffer. The past she represents is inexorable and merciless, controlling the present even when people think themselves most free. Her next scene, IV.iv, works in a similar but not identical way. In lines 1–7 she is again talking like a presenter of an interlude – a 'dire induction am I witness to' – moralizing and generalizing the play's action so far:

> So now prosperity begins to mellow
> And drop into the rotten mouth of death.

The fullness of time brings her curses to a grotesque fruition: the fruit falling of its own ripeness from the tree into the rotting mouth of the corpse at its foot. Again her first remarks are asides, pointing out the exactness of the parallel between what these women are suffering and what she has done. But by this time she is not alone in being a victim. She now joins with the other women in a formally patterned liturgy of lamentation and cursing, and this part of the scene, with her earlier appearance, forms a confine of lamentation, curse and prophecy round the central action of the play. Moreover, seeing the two Queens together is a neat visual symbol of the vicissitudes of Fortune and the illusory quality of all human expectation, be it that of a Margaret, a Clarence or a Richard; the old enemies are united by their fall, the two Queens have both come to ruin. The houses of York and Lancaster, which they embody, for the first time are united in common purpose: to curse, to blast the future.

Richard's sense of time is quite different. He sees the past as manipulatable in its relationship to the present:

> What though I killed her husband and her father?
> The readiest way to make the wench amends
> Is to become her husband and her father.

(I.i.154ff.)

He never quite loses this sense of past time being irrelevant to his present purpose:

> If I did take the kingdom from your sons,
> To make amends I'll give it to your daughter.

(IV.iv.294f.)

He has no sense of the past bearing on the present, of a chain of consequence and causality that limits present and future action. All things are in flux; even the things most resistant to him will yield to his will. (He is at least partly right: witness Anne.) It is noticeable that in his first soliloquy all the action of past and future is anchored by the tenses of the verbs to the present instant of his determination: the winter of discontent 'is' made glorious summer; he 'is' determined to prove a villain and to 'hate the idle pleasures of these days'. Yet in this present instant he is watching the coming to fruit of plans he laid in the past about the future 'Plots *have I laid* ... And if King Edward *be* as true and just ... This day *should* Clarence closely be mewed up ...' (32ff.). He seems to have the sense that time is his servant, that the event will vindicate him by allowing him to maintain his initiative and dominance. He is himself a symbol of distorted time, for even in infancy he rolled up the future into the present: he could 'gnaw a crust at two hours old', and is a monstrous incarnation of chaos, destroying the rootedness of civilization in sequential time where people conduct the present and plan for the future on the basis of the past. He is constantly appealing to a future time for satisfaction and justification: he will be King, he will marry Anne or Elizabeth, he will defeat Richmond. When Queen Elizabeth in IV.iv fights him on his own ground and takes away every value he could possibly and plausibly swear by, he is left with only one guarantee of his good faith, and it is no guarantee at all, since the judgement of good faith is based on experience not promise:

> What canst thou swear by now?
> The time to come.

But Elizabeth quickly replies,

> That thou hast wronged in the time o'er-past.
>
> (387)

Richard has failed to realize that the future is indivisible from the past and the present, and that what he has been makes him what he is and will be, setting limits, which get ever smaller, to his freedom. His past is physically represented on stage in the dream before Bosworth:

> Methought the souls of all that I had murdered
> Came to my tent, and every one did threat
> Tomorrow's vengeance on the head of Richard.
>
> (V.iii.205ff.)

His future now is one of no choice: 'I shall despair' (201).

The time to come has a nasty way of letting down those who take it for granted. Richard is let down by it; yet given what Shakespeare has made him it is difficult to see if he could have had any other ultimate value. For it is in the very nature of Machiavellian political ethics that the end is always one step ahead, justifying the means in the present.

Such an ethic looks to Fortune and the event to set things right, but is hopelessly dependent on the unpredictability of both. Machiavelli's own advice, all too true as regards public opinion, implies as much: 'The means will always be judged honourable *if* [my italics] the issue of the event is successful.' Whereas Margaret sees present suffering as justified and deserved in the past, Richard sees it as a road to a future that never comes, an infinite regress of expedient action. But men grow old and die. His philosophy does not square with the facts of life observable round him. He who rejects all values but the satisfaction of the will ends up unable to find meaning in anything, even in his own anguish before Bosworth. He who manipulated event in historical time ends up unable to see history as more than event infinitely extended. At least the other characters do see some meaning, do see time as having a logic leading to a nemesis where people get what they deserved and their true nature and state is revealed. Indeed, Margaret and Richmond see time in a prophetic, almost mystical, certainly providential way:

> Smile, heaven, upon this fair conjunction,
> That long have frowned upon their enmity . . .

(V.v.20ff.)

(One has to admit Richmond's expression is pretty perfunctory, not to say facile.) In some sense, therefore, the play is in some measure concerned with conflicting theories of history and politics. The model of the world one adopts affects conduct, which is judged by event; but one can never be quite sure the inference of that judgement is not coincidental, and so there can be no watertight proof of the nihilist model of Richard, the more hopeful one of Richmond, or of Margaret's terrible vision of endless chains of unexpiated guilt and suffering.

8. The Structure of the Play

Richard III is a very shapely play. It is built with a peculiarly neat and balanced structure, and the disposition of scenes and handling of character and incident indicate what type of interest Shakespeare had in his material. It is obvious, for example, that Richard and the progress of his career are the central areas of interest, and there are therefore few scenes in which he does not appear or, even if absent, dominate. Moreover, his character is so central to the play that a good number of characters are used to highlight him: Buckingham, for example, is another amoral politician on the make, who acts as a foil to Richard's own career and falls when events move outside his control; Clarence's recognition of his guilt, and the way he recognizes it, are, as we have seen, to be compared with Richard's; the divided voices of the Murderers pre-echo Richard's divided self in his dream before Bosworth. Even Margaret's recognition of pattern in the events of Richard's rise to power is linked to Richard's ironic sense of neatness, when he becomes husband and father to the woman whose husband and father he killed. Moreover, the handling of the Vice/Machiavel figure of Richard himself as hero dictates a structure that will at all points highlight him. The play's shape does this admirably, and suggests a type of response to him that is not immediately the most obvious given the Morality elements in it.

In Elizabethan theories of art it was axiomatic that the outward form ought to show the inner nature of things. The structure of plays, therefore, is likely to be intimately connected with what they are setting out to do and what category or genre they belong to.* Analysis of the shape of *Richard III* shows that the material of real history is being made into the accepted form for tragedy, and owes a lot to Senecan influence.† The action, as Aristotle had recommended and Seneca had practised, is single:

---

* Polonius in *Hamlet* II.2.379ff. is comically made to have aspirations to literary theory, and he recognizes not only 'history', but also 'historical-pastoral, tragical-historical, tragical-comical-historical-pastoral'; the joke against Polonius would lose its point if Shakespeare could not count on his audience recognizing that plays could be written in different modes and that those modes would carry certain expectations with them.

† Act divisions in printed texts are nearly always non-authorial afterthoughts, and are in any case imperceptible on stage without the massive punctuation marks of a drawing of the curtain or an interval. It is best to see Renaissance plays in performance as a sequence of scenes. Scenes themselves often break up into recognizable sections, as one or more characters enter or leave. (The fondness for five acts is an inheritance from Seneca.)

there is no subplot, and apart from the humour of Richard himself in aside and soliloquy there is no comic relief except in the scene with Clarence's murderers – and that is hardly worthy of the name, however much mileage actors seem in the early days to have got out of it. In a history play covering a good many years, the recommendation of the Italian critics that the action should deal only with the crisis of events and preferably within twenty-four hours is obviously an impossible requirement, but Time is deliberately foreshortened to give the illusion of events moving very fast indeed to their conclusion (see above, p. 35). As I said above, the movements of the play correspond closely to the recognized 'movements' of a Classical tragedy.

The play is hung round a number of balanced moments and scenes, where we get a sort of 'before and after' effect. The opening soliloquy in which Richard introduces himself has as its major note the idea of division, of Richard as an instrument of discord who hates this 'weak piping time of peace'; Richmond's final speech looks forward to reconciliation and harmony of warring factions through marriage. The wooing of Anne and the scene with Elizabeth where Richard seeks her daughter's hand are obviously linked in their style and manner, but also in the way their situations parallel and contrast. In the former, Richard interrupts a procession, thus breaking the ritual order that Anne is following, and woos her successfully in public; in the latter, it is Richard who is interrupted in his progress with his army by the three women, and the army remains on stage while Richard seeks the hand of Elizabeth unsuccessfully. In I.ii it is Anne who is tied in linguistic and rhetorical knots; in IV.iv despite his resourcefulness it is the Queen who fights Richard onto the ropes. Immediately after the wooing of Anne we have the scene where Margaret launches her grand curse, that each of its victims in the course of the play recognizes in the moment of its fulfilment; immediately before Richard's scene with the Queen the three women join in the ritual lamentation, recognizing the inheritance of guilt in which they all share, and calling for vengeance on Richard. Immediately after I.iii we see Clarence's death, the first of Richard's plots to come to fruition; immediately before the scene of lamentation, IV.iv, two short scenes highlight the last and most terrible of Richard's crimes, the murder of the Princes – the murdering of the innocent as Clarence's was the murdering of the guilty. The dying Edward's desire for reconciliation in II.i, thwarted by Richard's histrionic handling of the news of Clarence's death, is balanced in IV.i by a scene in which division of the family is explicit – mother from children, Queen from court into sanctuary, her son Dorset sent to join Stanley's son with the pretender to the throne. II.ii and III.v and vii contrast in a neat way: in the first, Clarence's children see through Richard's deceit, Edward's death is announced to formal lamentation, and Richard enters with Buckingham and others on a note of glutinous condolence: 'Sister, have comfort.' In III.v and vii Richard and Buckingham stage manage his appearance to the citizens as a holy and unambitious man in order to win popular support for his claim to the throne, Edward's life is traduced by them, and the citizens, as the Scrivener shows, are more than a little suspicious of recent events. And at the centre of the play is that block of scenes stretching from the arrival of the Princes to the fall of Hastings, where Richard's control of events is complete, his enemies, Rivers, Grey and Vaughan meet their deaths remembering Margaret's curse on them, and he makes the final moves preparatory to seizing the crown. The central scene of the play is the council scene of III.iv. Richard dominates the thoughts of others while he is absent; his late entry emphasizes his dominance; his return after consultation with Buckingham is to challenge the council to defy his power, and no one lifts a finger to save the overconfident Hastings despite the grossly incredible charge against him. As a central – and therefore, according to contemporary artistic theory in painting and poetry, crucial – scene this might look a little odd until we realize that firstly it is demonstrating Richard's complete dominance by force of will and desire of the assembled aristocracy, temporal and spiritual * of England, but also is the culmination of the little tragedy of Hastings who symbolizes in his folly, his self-indulgence, his willingness to rub along with Richard – and his blindness – an aristocracy that deserves such a King. There is no effective opposition to Richard. Shakespeare was not in a position to know the historical validity of such a suggestion; but the contemporary application of the history of Richard (see p. 27) certainly allows a contemporary inference to be drawn.

Seen from outside, then, the play certainly has a neatly symmetrical structure, balanced round a picture of Richard at his apogee. The parallels I have drawn could well be extended into greater detail. From the inside, as it were, the events are also seen to have a shape. For it is a play whose characters are peculiarly conscious of being in a process that has meaning. Some of them can see no further than a desire for revenge, a desire for a pattern of crude justice, and a satisfaction when they see it come – which, not unimportantly, is a sign of their spiritual illness, for that emotion is part of the Deadly Sin of Envy. Anne prays for vengeance

---

* Ely's eager bustling off to get strawberries is not only sycophantic; it is a deserting of proper concerns in a moment of high importance. He goes, moreover, because Richard pretends to want something to eat – his appetite again (see p. 107).

in I.ii, Margaret in I.iii; the Queen's call for vengeance on Richard in IV.i and IV.iv; the ghosts of those he murdered threaten him in V.iii. Moreover, the play is very full of omens and portents that are recognized as such: Clarence's prophetic dream is a fine example. Omens surround the Princes, the children of an impious race, as they go to the Tower, and Hastings is met out of nowhere by a pursuivant sharing a name with him, a sort of *doppelgänger*, to whom he recalls in false confidence the last time they met – on his way to the Tower. Richard himself is not only aware of omens – the similarity in sound of 'Richmond' and 'Rougemont' – but is treated to the biggest helping of the lot in the parade of the vindictive ghosts the night before Bosworth. Moreover, he is himself the biggest portent of them all – a child who upset all the rules of normal development, an unnatural son, brother, husband. And then there is Margaret, the personification, almost as a type of Fury, of past crime and guilt unhistorically present in this action. (Richard is made to stress the *surprise* of seeing her I.iii.166ff.) She constantly and mercilessly points out to the sufferers that they are getting exactly what they deserve; for her, history is as exact a balance as we have seen the shape of the play to be. These hints of dim foreknowing, reinforced by our historical knowledge as audience, coupled with the obvious pattern of the disposition of scenes, strongly suggest a controlling Providence in human affairs analogous to the control of the playwright in his play.

Shakespeare's control over how he writes the play is, of course, total. The symmetrical structure suggests a deep interest in the rise and fall of Richard, and everything else I have said above suggests a focusing on him and his significance. When we notice that the play's four natural movements do in fact match very closely the four-part structure regarded as peculiarly satisfying and shapely in Classical tragedy, the conclusion becomes irresistible that Shakespeare was asking us, at least on one level, to look at Richard as a tragic hero on the Senecan model: the man of enormous and perverted ability, the bloody tyrant, whose fall is nevertheless terrible and cataclysmic. In Scaliger's terminology, the *protasis* of a play is the first part, where characters are introduced. In this play there is a lot of material to be resumed from the *Henry VI* plays, and Shakespeare has to prepare for the new material and emphases. We might see this as running from I.i to I.iv. The *epitasis* is where the plot thickens – say from II.i to III.iv. The *catastasis*, where the action is fully wound up, and begins to turn round to catastrophe, runs from III.v to the point where Richard is simultaneously at the height of his power and beginning to lose control of events, IV.iv. The *catastrophe* – the denouement, the final event of the dramatic progression – is dealt with from V.i to V.iii, where Richard meets his end fighting with a gallantry as conspicuous as that of Richmond was circumspect.*

To handle this structure with the obvious, almost bravura, confidence Shakespeare shows in the writing of this play argues a good deal of deep thought and study about the nature and theory of drama. It also argues a good knowledge of Seneca and what other playwrights and critics – like Heywood, Marlowe and Kyd – were making of him in English conditions. We have no knowledge whatsoever of when or how Shakespeare could have subjected himself to such a course of study; but the evidence for his interest in the theory of drama is pretty strong in all his work, and it would be dangerous to dismiss out of hand the idea that part of the subject of *Richard III* is the nature of drama itself and its relation to the shape of events in real life. (Simply the number of references in the play to acting and illusion would tend to support this anyway.) Clearly, the world/stage metaphor is never far from the surface, but I think Shakespeare's concern becomes rather more specialized than this important inclusive metaphor, without for one minute ignoring it.

It seems to me that there is a good case for seeing Shakespeare's interest as lying first of all in Richard as a tragic hero who exemplifies the desire for power and is judged, and found wanting, by his handling of it. The play is a study of power. Richard rises to a position of power through his own remarkable qualities and then precipitates a national convulsion by his fall as a result of those same qualities. He, and most of his victims, show what the appetite for power can do to a man. But he is an odd tragic hero, for he is the comic Vice hybridized with the sinister and dangerous Machiavel, and his criminality is apparently used by Providence as a way of cleaning up the world's accumulated crime. Thus while he is tragic, he is comic too – which takes us back to the idea of farce I discussed above (see p. 56). Therefore, it seems that part of the subject of the play must also be the meaning of historical suffering and the nature of a Providence that uses evil to purge evil. Yet it is undeniable that at the end of the play we do have more than a hint of the true tragic feeling that something of value has been lost, that human potential has been wasted and man's dignity somehow vindicated – which we could not have if the play could be reduced to the Morality level my last sentence suggested. Possibly, in creating a Senecan tragic hero for a play set in a Christian England, Shakespeare is beginning to ask a question I think he returns to, and answers, in *Macbeth*, a play obviously related to this one: is tragedy, that affirmation of human dignity and value in the

---

* A similar four-part structure is used in *Macbeth* and *Coriolanus*.

face of terrible and irrevocable destruction, possible in a Christian context, where, as Lady Julian of Norwich so movingly put it, ultimately all shall be well, all manner of thing shall be well?

9. Language, Style and Rhetoric

Anyone with even half an ear will notice that the language of this play is remarkably patterned. It is not just a question of the rapid exchange of similar sentence structures employing similar words in the tense stichomthyic exchanges between Richard and Anne, for example, or the formal and patterned echoing of words and ideas in the mourning and cursing of the three women. The play throughout is full of elaborate rhetorical patterns of high artificiality which deliberately draw attention to themselves: how a thing is said becomes part of what is said. Moreover, Shakespeare has clearly given characters differing modes of articulation and expression, from the comic mock-logic of the murderers, through the extreme rationality of Richard's disputes, to the extended metaphors and conceits of, for example, Clarence's dream. It is also very noticeable that except when he is playing for an effect, or parodying, Richard's language is almost devoid of imagery and metaphor, whereas his victims and Richmond employ a wealth of personification of abstract ideas and values and attach a great deal of metaphor to Richard himself. The fact that the major mode of any play's discourse is its language means that this problem cannot be ignored.

We need briefly to glance at contemporary attitudes to language and to rhetoric, the means of using it to best effect. In my *Shakespeare's History Plays* I have examined in some detail the Renaissance debate about the nature of language: whether it was only a convention, so that words designated things merely by habit and custom and did not organically relate to their inner nature, and thus could convey only a limited or relative truth, or whether, on the other hand, it could convey truths which were universal. It is obvious that this debate relates intimately to discussion of the nature of human knowledge and the possibility of it being more than provisional. These worries – which are with us today – were by no means only the business of the learned, and the exploitation of ambiguity in, for example, pun, irony and *double entendre* in writing (including plays) which is a notable feature of English Renaissance style is clear evidence that language and its relation to truth (what truth?) is a concern in many people's minds. The discourse of a play, which as a whole is itself a metaphor, does not exploit metaphor and imagery merely for fun: such a style defines the reality the speaker sees and judges it against that which the audience perceives.

If language itself is an issue, it follows that the ways in which it can be consciously deployed and used were too. Francis Bacon (and others) made a distinction between the use of language in rigorously logical discourse, in dialectic, to convince and prove, and the more emotive and attractive deployment of it to move, please and persuade in rhetoric: echoing a cliché from Antiquity, the one was compared to the power of the closed fist that compelled, the other to the grace of the open hand that greeted, inviting the reader's or hearer's agreement. Bacon, again representatively, says that the use of the former mode is best confined to a learned audience; for the vast majority of people, the rhetorical mode is the most efficient manner of discourse.

Nowadays we often forget that in the sixteenth century rhetoric was an admired and nearly universal skill. The number of technical books published on the subject was, without any overstatement, huge, and we may be quite sure that each copy had a good number of readers. The manuals of rhetoric aimed to teach their users how to write and speak powerfully by employing the recognized tropes and figures* whose effectiveness and appropriateness had been endlessly discussed and analysed since Antiquity. In *Richard III*, as in his other work, Shakespeare shows thorough familiarity with the techniques of rhetoric, and it is possible to dig out from the play examples of very many figures, however complex.†

---

* Tropes and figures are both deliberate deviations from the norm of plain communication. A trope is a change or transference of the meaning of words, for example in metaphor, allegory, irony, hyperbole, synecdoche or metonymy. The figures, on the other hand, may also be changes of meaning, but also are the different shapes or structural patterns into which they may be put. See next footnote.
† It may be helpful to give some examples of the figures from the play. The function of the figures will then be clearly apparent.

Anadiplosis – the same word in the last position in one clause and the first or near the first in the following clause. It suggests a causal connection: IV.iii.51–3:

> . . . I have learned that fearful commenting
> Is leaden servitor to dull delay;
> Delay leads impotent and snail-paced beggary.

(Anadiplosis continued through three or more clauses gives *climax* or *gradatio* – V.iii.194–6:

> My conscience hath a thousand several tongues,
> And every tongue brings in a several tale,
> And every tale condemns me for a villain.)

Anaphora – beginning lines or clauses with the same word or words, for emphasis or cumulative effect: I.ii.121–2:

Language, Style and Rhetoric

(*footnote cont.*)

> Your beauty was the cause of that effect –
> Your beauty, that did haunt me in my sleep . . .

(Often used with *parison* – see below.)

Antimetabole – inverted order, stressing a strong contrast: I.iii.71–2:

> Since every Jack became a gentleman
> There's many a gentle person made a Jack.

Epistrophe – the same word ending a sequence, used to stress the important word or idea: I.i.55–8:

> And from the cross-row plucks the letter G,
> And says a wizard told him that by G
> His issue disinherited should be.
> And, for my name of George begins with G . . .

Epizeuxis – a more stressed form of *ploce* (see below), where the word is repeated without any other word intervening: III.iii.8:

> O Pomfret, Pomfret . . .

Isocolon – exactly the same length to corresponding clauses, to achieve stress or emphasis or contrast: II.ii.82–5:

> She for an Edward weeps, and so do I;
> I for a Clarence weeps, so doth not she;
> These babes for Clarence weep, and so do I;
> I for an Edward weep, so do not they.

Parison – parallel grammatical structure: III.iii.17–18:

> Then cursed she Richard, then cursed she Buckingham,
> Then cursed she Hastings.

Ploce – repeating a word within the same clause or line: II.iv.62–3:

> Make war upon themselves, brother to brother,
> Blood to blood, self against self.

Then there are the various types of ambiguity:

Antanaclasis – a sort of pun, repeating a word and shifting its meaning: I.ii.15, where the double play is on 'art' ('heart'/'art' was a common pun, as the 'h' was unaspirated at the time.):

> Cursèd the heart that had the heart to do it!

Asteismus – where a word is returned to the speaker by his interlocutor with an unexpected second meaning: 'naught' in I.i.97–8.

> With this, my lord, myself have naught to do.
> Naught to do with Mistress Shore?

Paronomasia – a sort of pun, repeating a word similar in sound to one already used: IV.iv.415:

> Not my deserts, but what I will deserve.

We might dismiss this as merely one of those historical accidents that may be interesting but do not affect how we read the play, but to do this would be a serious mistake. Our age has little or none of this technical knowledge and appreciation I have outlined, and so when we come across an epanalepsis, say, we may simply touch our hats to it and pass on – if we recognize it at all. But Shakespeare's audience – or at least a good proportion of it – would have had a highly technical understanding of the resources of rhetoric, and would have noticed how these figures, each with its own particular function, were being used or misused in their context.* This becomes very important when the context is a play. The audience is being persuaded to accept its illusion by the rhetoric of the play as a whole, while part of the business of that illusion is to watch and judge how inside it one character manipulates language to persuade another and how their self-expression defines what they are. Demanding attention to the technicalities of language is therefore one of Shakespeare's ways of controlling and directing our response to his people. Moreover, as we have seen, the problem with persuasive and metaphorical language is how far it relates to truth, and to what sort of truth. Thus awareness of how language is being used converges with all the other ways in which an audience is directed to look at the central issues expressed within and by the fiction of the play.

A play is at bottom a narrative. But simply by its being presented as an illusion of historic time, in the interplay of characters and what they say, an audience is precluded from valuing that narrative entirely objectively. Further, within the verbal texture of the play certain ideas and concepts may recur so often that, insignificant in each separate mention, they come cumulatively to set the atmosphere for it. This will subliminally affect an audience's response and sympathy and recognition of certain important thematic ideas. In this play the very first lines

---

Polyptoton – a repetition of a word-root with different inflection or ending (another sort of pun): I.ii.7:

> Thou bloodless remnant of that royal blood

Syllepsis – yet another way of exploiting ambiguity, where a word carries two meanings but is not repeated: I.i.115:

> I will deliver you, or else lie for you.

* Even a modern audience is unable to miss how the contrasting speeches of Brutus and Antony after Caesar's death in *Julius Caesar* exploit different modes of rhetoric whose technicalities as well as their effects convey to us a lot about the speakers, their attitudes to their audiences, their assessment of their situation and the nature of their relationship to Caesar and what they saw him standing for.

introduce the idea of storm and bad weather, momentarily suspended, but menacing the house of York and, by extension, that of England. That image is rapidly drawn into a complex centring round the notion of gardens, trees, orchards, agriculture. The royal house is seen as a tree shaken by storms (I.i.1ff. and I.iii.259); Edward is 'The royal tree [who] hath left us royal fruit' (IIII.vii.166, said ironically by Richard of Edward's children); but on the 'royal stock' 'ignoble plants' have been 'grafted' (III.vii.126 – Buckingham on Edward's marriage to Elizabeth Woodville; cf. 215). When Edward dies, the Queen laments 'Why grow the branches when the root is gone? Why wither not the leaves that want their sap?' (II.ii.41–2). Weeds and flowers (which have not yet fruited) are the ambiguous – for which is which depends on point of view – analogues of the Princes and Richard in II.iv.13ff. Gardens, orchards or woods – all needing management and cultivation, all subject to the vagaries of the uncontrollable weather, all needing to breed true to produce good fruit – are constantly kept in mind. Even little touches like the Citizen's remarks in II.iii.32ff. keep alive the idea of an orchard subject to the cycle of the seasons and the vulnerability of the undergrowth to the fall of a great tree:

> When clouds are seen, wise men put on their cloaks;
> When great leaves fall, then winter is at hand;
> When the sun sets, who doth not look for night?
> Untimely storms make men expect a dearth.

The parison and anaphora of the first three lines not only makes memorable the three related ideas expressed in almost proverbial pithiness, but also by stressing the word 'when' emphasizes the link between the political process and seasonal change; and the little people can do as much about the one as they can about the other. This strain of imagery running through the play suggests a theme that links it with *Richard II*: the management of the garden that fallen man as a result of his sin now has to cultivate. This image is one of the oldest ways of describing and evaluating the process of politics, and carries with it the inescapable memory both of the Eden man lived in before the Fall and of the toil and sorrow to which his sin condemned him.

Another set of defining and atmospheric images relates to Richard. No character in the entire Shakespeare canon is more consistently compared to the brutes that want discourse of reason – and, of course, the choice of those comparisons throws light on those who so compare him. He is a sheep-worrying dog, a 'hellhound' (Margaret, IV.iv.48), a biting, venom-toothed dog – i.e. a mad dog (Margaret again, I.iii.290);

his physical appearance suggesting his inner moral nature is neatly summed up in 'elvish-marked, abortive, rooting hog' (Margaret yet again, I.iii.227); comparing him to a 'bottled spider' (Margaret, I.iii.241) suggests both his poison and – to us – the cleverness of the webs in which he has trapped his victims. He is a 'poisonous bunch-backed toad' (Margaret, I.iii.245; cf. Anne, I.ii.147), a 'deadly boar', (Stanley, IV.v.2), a 'foul swine' (Richmond, V.ii.10; cf. V.ii.7: Richard's crest was a boar). We should not see these creatures as merely nonce-correlatives for Richard, of no significance; for in a world where everything signified something beyond itself, animals carried a wealth of symbolism. It is perhaps significant, for example, that Richmond twice in three lines compares the man he is fighting for possession of the throne to the crest that would identify him and his party in battle: the implication is that he has descended to the nature of the thing that is his badge. Moreover, all these animal comparisons are highly relevant to ideas we have seen are associated with Richard. The toad is traditionally associated with the devil, particularly when he first tempted Eve,* and with the sin of greed or avarice; the spider is again associated with the Devil who maliciously weaves his webs to trap men, and with the sin of avarice that bleeds its victims dry. The hog or pig is a symbol of greed, gluttony and lust – and these sins are explicitly connected with Richard (on gluttony, see below). While the dog is most often a symbol of faithfulness, it can also, depending on context, be a symbol of envy. Most of the animals to which Richard is compared – the dog, the boar, the wolf – have associations with violence. The vast majority of these animal comparisons which value and qualify our perception of Richard are given to the woman who in her person and presence in the play personifies the violence and suffering of the past that has reached a terrible harvest in the career of Richard.

Through the imagery applied to him we are not only given suggestions about Richard's symbolic relationships which are convergent with the implications we have already discussed of his dramatic ancestry, but we are also made to see his crooked figure as a physically manifest image that is a summation of the world others have made. Richard himself, as physical presence and as amoral agent, is the central and final symbol, the icon and epitome of what the Wars of the Roses have inexorably led up to. He is the King who expresses both the sin and the deserts of

---

* Compare Milton, *Paradise Lost*, IV.800, and Pope, *Epistle to Arbuthnot*, 319–20:

> Or at the ear of Eve, familiar Toad,
> Half froth, half venom, spits himself abroad.

England, the (unwitting) scourge of God who is almost a scapegoat. The irony of his not realizing how he is being used, and the logic of history behind him and creating the conditions in which he can be as he is, must increase the possibility of sympathy for him.

Comparing him to beasts links to his Machiavellianism as well. It was a cliché of the period that the Machiavellian Prince had surrendered to the fulfilment of his sensual and sinful passions, and in so doing had allowed what was bestial in him to dominate the reason that made him a man; the beast became his true model. Richard explicitly identifies himself as a Machiavel, and the beast imagery attached to him is a way of reinforcing and illustrating this self-presentation by the way he is perceived by other people, who, by definition, cannot know he is a Machiavel. Moreover, the surrender to desire and appetite for its own sake – for Richard has no idea what to do with the power he covets – is interestingly emphasized by the connection of Richard with food. Notice how frequently supper or meals are mentioned before or after his crimes: he becomes a glutton for blood. In almost the same breath as the casual answer, 'Chop off his head,' to Buckingham's inquiry about what to do if Hastings will not be a party to the plot, Richard suggests, 'Come, let us sup betimes, that afterwards We may digest our complots in some form' (III.i.193–200). The plot becomes a post-prandial delight. Similarly, at IV.iii.31ff., Tyrrel is ordered to come to Richard immediately after the main meal and over the dessert to tell him all the details of the murder of the Princes. Most striking of all, Richard's first crime, the murder of Clarence, is the only one of which we see any details of the execution. Clarence is literally made into a sop, a piece of bread or cake soaked in wine as a breakfast or supper dish. The murderers make the point explicitly (I.iv.159ff.). The imagery of food, appearing at these crucial points, underlines Richard's *appetite*: his unbridled desire. The rehearsal of all the old images of order and disorder in Ulysses' speech in *Troilus and Cressida* which I quoted above (p. 7), concludes:

> And appetite, an universal wolf,
> So doubly seconded with will and power,
> Must make perforce an universal prey,
> And last eat up himself.

Richard is that universal wolf, who makes a prey of all his world, and at the end destroys himself by being divided into nonentity in his very soul. The imagery, far from being merely illustrative, has most economically directed our intuitive understanding to a proper, and properly complex, assessment of Richard.

The Machiavellian denies all abstract ideals and values except effectiveness. This must imply a good deal for the language and style he can properly use. For Richard, the values – however topsy-turvy – by which others act in the play are mere words, mere air, signifying nothing: conscience itself is a word whose only referent is to the solipsism of the coward who uses it as justification for his cowardice (V.iii.310). He juggles terms that relate to even basic human alliances and relationships, like 'husband' and 'father', until they are meaningless. But the inner core of meaninglessness is masked deliberately by the essential tool of the villain: the ability to persuade. Richard's acting exploits as many different styles as he has roles. He can appear bluff and blunt; he can adopt the high speech of a King; he can play with the speech of a lover, and imitate the cadences of the divine. Since we know from the opening address to the audience what he is and what lies, or does not lie, at the heart, we cannot but pay attention to these differing styles as styles, and assess their effectiveness in a given situation and with a given audience. In Richard, a man to whom rhetoric is a tool to the achievement of an end, we are seeing a virtuoso display of the art of rhetoric. We are seeing just how effective and at the same time how dangerous a tool it can be. It is perhaps for this reason that the flatness of Richmond's final speech is almost refreshing.

Richard's extreme self-consciousness about his acting and his deployment of language is further exemplified by the complex blend of double meanings he addresses as much to his own perception of his own wit as it is to (for example) Clarence – 'I will deliver you, or else lie for you' – or to the appreciative audience he assumes. He is aware that the meaning of what he says is in some measure defined by the hearer and the situation. He makes cruel fun of how people receive and understand speech and language. Up to a point, we share his amusement, for like the Bastard in *King John*, he makes the traditional relationships of the world of moral order, and the words in which they are expressed seem illusory, ambiguous and even comic. Richard, again like the Bastard, and like Edmund in *King Lear*, is fascinated by dissimulation and domination, like them conscious not just of his situational but of his perceptual difference from his fellows. Rejection of old beliefs and new faith in their own self is the basis of the temporary success of this type of man, the Machiavellian, whom Donne, in Sermon LXXX, defines as the 'natural' as opposed to the Christian man, who rejects his religious and ethical past and everything else that is not demonstrably of the world and of the present – including the significance of linguistic terms that cannot be directly quantified.

Yet the world Richard lives in – and by extension the political and moral world in which real live Elizabethan Machiavels were believed to be operating – is not so simple; it turns round and bites him. Playing rhetorically and cynically with terms whose reality he does not accept, he is eventually trapped by the fact that others do accept them, and can *cooperate through speech* to achieve his downfall. Even where he was most secure, in his grasp of himself, he finds the reality of the conscience he denied is far from illusory. So in one sense the comedy of the play turns on the foolishness of extreme cleverness, on the capacity of language to evaluate and to trap its user.

Richard's different styles, precisely because they are recognizable as rhetorical modes of particular application, necessarily evaluate him as he uses them. Generally, Shakespeare uses styles to express a way of perceiving – the style of Tyrrel responding to the Princes' murder tells us a lot about Tyrrel as well as about the murder itself, and the argument between Clarence's murderers shows two men of relatively simple mind trying to get to grips with an issue that is too big for them to analyse properly in the language available to them. Styles are thus an important device for differentiating characters – and for showing their convergence. For example, in Margaret's first appearance she is isolated, and her style is sharply distinguished in its formal patterning from that of those who turn on her. But when her curses are being fulfilled, the styles the Queen and the Duchess of York use in IV.iv are almost identical to hers. And in that ritualistic utterance, an antiphonal patterned chorus of despair and hate, the three women sink their individuality. But as they do so something interesting seems to happen, which I think we are meant to notice: they are redefining real suffering and murder through expression in a formal, patterned, elevated style so that the rawness can be accommodated, part-neutralized in ceremony. But this is ultimately to shirk the issue of the *meaning* of that suffering and crime. (We see something of the same thing, I feel, in the verbal fireworks of Anne's lament for Henry in I.ii.) It arrests it in a memory of the past that can only be vindictive, refuses to face it in its naked chaos and digest it so that there is a possibility of new growth. That crime and the suffering it engenders is embodied in Richard, rationalist causer of an anti-rational chaos, who presents and focuses for us the central enigmas of the play: the relation of crime to punishment, the past to the future, the evil agent to the providential purpose. The women, like him, are living, in many senses, in a world of words, and one of the issues the play is deeply concerned with is the relation of words to the real parameters of human existence and human politics and the law of God.

Afterword

Richard III was an immediate success, and remained so even when its topicality had evaporated. Its quality was self-evident – a play of such bravura writing and construction that it would be difficult to cut a line without serious distortion. (Which did not stop Colley Cibber mauling and butchering it in his reworked, shorter version that was the only one performed between 1700 and 1877.) But, as we have seen, its initial popularity must in some measure have been due to its handling of pressing contemporary concerns; it is after all a play built not only on a personal but also a public interest in political morality and the nature of power. The presentation of the career of a Richard who, to Elizabethan eyes, is historically entirely credible, offered a workable myth to examine the challenge to the idea of a world of political and moral order presented by an anarchic egotism. It raises, too, a major theological issue of extreme contemporary interest: an age that was so theologically literate that one might very well have to discuss Calvin's doctrine of election or the nature of the sacraments while having one's hair cut was more than just interested in the issues of free will, the nature and origin of evil and the way in which the Providence of God interacted with human beings. These were open questions, furiously and ceaselessly discussed – and fought over with guns and swords. The malignity of Richard, and his career, clearly involves them.

It obviously would cast a strange light over the play if it were to be approached from a position that saw all human beings as from before their birth either damned to Hell or elected to the glory of Heaven, and incapable of affecting the issue either way.* God's Mercy, Evil and the Devil himself in this climate inevitably become pressing topics for discussion, and it is noticeable that in the years around 1600 there are a large number of plays that either feature Machiavels, or examine the nature of evil, or have 'a devil in them'. (Ben Jonson complained that no play would 'take' without one.) Shakespeare himself keeps returning to the issue of evil and its parasitic relationship to good: Aaron in *Titus Andronicus*, Don John in *Much Ado about Nothing*, Iago in *Othello*, Edmund in *King Lear* – and, supremely, Macbeth. And he never loses sight of the issue of Free Will that is closely connected to it.

---

* The strict Calvinist position, which is implied in Articles X and XVII of the Church of England. It is doubtful whether Shakespeare took this view; *Macbeth* or *Hamlet*, for example, seem to take a much more Roman Catholic position. (John Speed, in 1611, said that Shakespeare was a 'Papist'.)

But Shakespeare could hardly have written *Macbeth*, or *Richard III* for that matter, without having taken into account the work of Marlowe. In several of his plays Marlowe had examined in figures like the Guise, Barabas or Tamburlaine, the murderous Machiavellian superman, delighting in his own clever evil, who overreaches himself to his own ruin. In Richard Shakespeare embodied all the energies of this sort of hero, but related them, as Marlowe never did, to the positives that spring from an acknowledgement of conscience, of the idea of Providence, of pity and compassion. Richard is surrounded by people who cry for justice (however limited their view of it) when he for the greater part of the play implicitly denies the meaningfulness of the word; by people who recognize their own guilt and their own deservings when he can only use such concepts to play linguistic games to deceive his victims. The advance is well illustrated by comparing Shakespeare's treatment of Clarence, who though a sinner is given a fair measure of our pity and a recognition of justice, with Marlowe's handling of the cold callousness of the treatment meted out to the innocent Bajazeth in Part One of *Tamburlaine the Great*: there is no pity for him, but instead an almost sadistic glee in his suffering. *Richard III* shows how Shakespeare's response to Marlowe had crystallized in a much more penetrating examination of the Machiavellian hero and his context. Together with what Keats called the 'negative capability' of penetrating and creating credibly the consciousness of a man wedded to evil, so that we as audience can feel what it would be like to be Richard, goes something Marlowe never even attempted: a concurrent awareness of the dynamics of the moral universe in which he myopically bustles, which goes far beyond the mere irony that results from knowing what historically happened to him. It is just this double focus that bears such remarkable fruit in *Macbeth*.

We have already noticed how Richard's, and before him Clarence's, discovery of conscience anticipates, is almost a sketch for, Macbeth's self-perception. (Shakespeare even uses the same device of sickening seesaw rhythms in the verse.) In *Macbeth* Shakespeare returns to the problem of evil, its ultimate sterility, the paradox that when the will is given free rein it progressively *reduces* the sinner's freedom. But whereas Richard's career in the play must be seen – in however complex a sense – as comic, Macbeth's cannot: in his play not only is the inner Hell Richard merely glimpsed too powerfully realized in all its isolation and sterility, but also the moment of Macbeth's desperate choice is too finely balanced. Richard, *ex hypothesi*, never had a choice whether or not to be a villain; Macbeth has a completely free one, and nearly chooses not to be. There Shakespeare's interest lies not in a man who from the outset is 'determined to prove a villain', but in a good and noble soldier whose fatal choice of his own self-will and ambition against his better judgement destroys him. It is precisely those qualities that made him 'noble Macbeth', that make it possible for him to turn into a 'hellhound': the higher up the ladder men are, the more devastating their fall. As the old proverb has it, *corruptio optima pessima* – 'the corruption of the best makes the worst.' Moreover, Macbeth's self-consciousness makes him know exactly what he is doing and what is happening to him, and despairingly face the irony that the route he took to the kingship put all that made that kingship worth having beyond his reach. Macbeth is no Machiavel, no Vice like Richard, where we have to start with the *donnée* that ultimately his evil is inexplicable. It is all too explicable. Further, whereas in *Richard III* we are never allowed to forget that Richard is operating in a recent historical context, and therefore we have to see him with the detachment and irony that context implies, *Macbeth* is located in a remote, legendary time so that Shakespeare can look hard, almost singlemindedly, at the inner sensibility and self-destructiveness of the man who chooses evil.

Shakespeare's continuing interest in the problem of evil takes into account, as it must, that if evil were not attractive *even when we know it is evil*, it would be powerless. The devil can indeed appear as an angel of light – as Richard reminds us; he can cite Scripture to his own purpose – as Richard does. But he fools few, and those who consent to him in the play – Buckingham, Hastings, Tyrrel, the murderers – know exactly what they are doing. But what about the audience? For the whole play is built on the premise that they will find Richard attractive.

Indeed, one of the issues raised by the play concerns not only the illusion Richard creates among his victims, but the illusion that makes us respond to him as a person. That appearance of reality, even when we take into account the distancing effect of the ironies that surround him and are even implicit in his own language, poses a moral question of some importance to us: we consent to his evil and even share some of his exhilaration. We find ourselves enjoying vicariously, even admiring and envying, his evil cleverness. And when we feel that sense of loss at his end, a sense of something in him that if not admirable is at least compellingly interesting (as in Milton's Satan), it is disturbing to realize how deeply we have been attracted to what is after all unambiguous, self-declared evil. No Vice ever took an audience for such a ride. The play forces us to examine not just our politics and our understanding of Providence, but our own wills. When we do so, we find that the evil Richard expresses so powerfully finds its echo in us. He is dangerous; so, potentially, are we.

Appendices

The Text of the Play

Some of Shakespeare's contemporaries in the working theatre – for example Ben Jonson, in 1616 – took the trouble to see to the publication of volumes of their collected works in the large and dignified Folio format, sometimes with grandiose title pages that argue their sense of the importance of their work. Shakespeare never did; the first collected edition of his plays appeared in Folio in 1623, seven years after his death. His friends and business associates Heming and Condell saw it through the press, and made some effort to establish a reputable text for the work of one who was already recognized as England's finest dramatist. They are thus the first in a long line of editors who have wrestled with the peculiar problems the text of Shakespeare presents. *Richard III* is one of the most difficult examples, and to understand why this is so some explanation of the usual career of a text is needed.

What little evidence we have suggests that Shakespeare wrote the plays out in full. The chronology of the plays suggests he worked at great speed, under pressure. (Fast handwriting of the period can be very difficult indeed to read.) When the play went into rehearsal, separate parts, with cues, would be copied out for each actor to learn; and the copying introduces a possibility of error. The whole text would serve as a prompt book, and might well be scribbled over or changed in the light of modifications made when it was seen how it worked on the stage. Indeed, we ought perhaps to recognize that the original author's text merely serves as a baseline for the cooperative creation of the play in the theatre: the exigencies of performances would almost certainly lead to modifications in which the author would have an important hand and sometimes – *King Lear* might be an example – the changes are quite radical and lead to much loss of hair by textual critics attempting to decide what Shakespeare wrote. This is particularly true of a play, like *Richard III*, that was regularly performed for a good many years; even actors leaving the company might call for changes to be made in the text, for Shakespeare clearly wrote his parts with people he knew in mind to play them.

A good play was a valuable property. If it was a success, Shakespeare's company drew crowds away from the rival playhouses, and he was able to salt away a few more coins towards the purchase of New Place in

Stratford. The last thing a company would want, in an age before copyright or royalty laws, was for a text, particularly of a new play, to become available for general reading or even rival performance, because receipts would drop. But by the same token, there was a market for texts, and cheap quarto editions do appear of a good number of Shakespeare's plays.

An enterprising printer might commission a shorthand writer to attend the play and take it down from the performance. The resulting 'reported' play would obviously be full of errors, as well as divergences from Shakespeare's text caused not only by usual directorial handling, including cutting, of a text in performance, but also by the liberties taken with it by the actors – especially prone to this, as Hamlet's speech to the players indicates, were the popular clowns. One of the actors might be persuaded, for a consideration, to check it, but would probably know only his own part accurately. It might be such a travesty of the original that the company would be compelled to authorize a printing themselves, and here the copy text might be an illegible and annotated prompt book. Another reason for the appearance of quarto printings could well have been that when a play began to go out of fashion and ceased to be a major and jealously guarded draw, the company decided that a small profit from selling it to a bookseller was better than no profit at all. When these quartos were in print, of course, they could themselves serve as the company's prompt books, and more scribbles might again be added. Moreover, further printings of the quartos, which for various practical and legal reasons had to be set up in type by hand afresh on each occasion, would often use as copy text one or more of the previous printings. The possibility of error creeping in is already huge, and that is to say nothing of the demonstrable inaccuracy of some of the compositors who worked on the printings.

There are six quartos known of *Richard III*, one of the most popular of Shakespeare's plays. It has been suggested that the first Quarto, of 1597, is a 'reported' text, but this has been challenged. It is now seen to be probable that the manuscript from which it was set was a collective reconstruction – remarkably accurate – of the play from memory by most if not all the members of the company, and this would preserve not only inaccuracies and improvisation but deliberate alterations to the text after Shakespeare gave it to the company. (If this is so, it should be recalled that Shakespeare as working actor as well as playwright may well have had a hand in some of the alterations.) The first Quarto is the basis of the five quartos that follow, and by the time we get to Q6 a lot of mistakes have been amassed. The Folio printing was set mainly from

Q6, but the editors had access to part at least of Shakespeare's 'foul papers', and 190 lines were included that are in none of the quartos. To make matters even more difficult, some 500 lines (III.i.1–158, V.iii.49 to the end) were set from Q3 of 1602, which is derived from Q1; and the collator of the material was not the most efficient of readers. We therefore have a situation where when Q1 and Folio agree in a reading, we cannot check it at all, and the only part of the play which we can be fairly sure is as Shakespeare wrote it originally are the 190 lines peculiar to the Folio. The basis of a modern text therefore has to be Folio, but none of the quartos can be wholly ignored.

Richard's Soliloquies from *3 Henry VI*

III.ii.124–95

RICHARD

> Ay, Edward will use women honourably.
> Would he were wasted, marrow, bones, and all,
> That from his loins no hopeful branch may spring,
> To cross me from the golden time I look for!
> And yet, between my soul's desire and me –
> The lustful Edward's title burièd –
> Is Clarence, Henry, and his son young Edward,   130
> And all the unlooked-for issue of their bodies,
> To take their rooms, ere I can place myself:
> A cold premeditation for my purpose!
> Why then, I do but dream on sovereignty;
> Like one that stands upon a promontory
> And spies a far-off shore where he would tread,
> Wishing his foot were equal with his eye,
> And chides the sea that sunders him from thence,
> Saying he'll lade it dry to have his way;
> So do I wish the crown, being so far off;   140
> And so I chide the means that keeps me from it;
> And so I say I'll cut the causes off,
> Flattering me with impossibilities.
> My eye's too quick, my heart o'erweens too much,
> Unless my hand and strength could equal them.
> Well, say there is no kingdom then for Richard,
> What other pleasure can the world afford?
> I'll make my heaven in a lady's lap,

And deck my body in gay ornaments,
150 And 'witch sweet ladies with my words and looks.
O, miserable thought! And more unlikely
Than to accomplish twenty golden crowns!
Why, love forswore me in my mother's womb;
And, for I should not deal in her soft laws,
She did corrupt frail nature with some bribe
To shrink mine arm up like a withered shrub;
To make an envious mountain on my back,
Where sits deformity to mock my body;
To shape my legs of an unequal size;
160 To disproportion me in every part,
Like to a chaos, or an unlicked bear-whelp
That carries no impression like the dam.
And am I then a man to be beloved?
O, monstrous fault, to harbour such a thought!
Then, since this earth affords no joy to me
But to command, to check, to o'erbear such
As are of better person than myself,
I'll make my heaven to dream upon the crown,
And, whiles I live, t'account this world but hell,
170 Until my misshaped trunk that bears this head
Be round impalèd with a glorious crown.
And yet I know not how to get the crown,
For many lives stand between me and home;
And I – like one lost in a thorny wood,
That rents the thorns and is rent with the thorns,
Seeking a way and straying from the way,
Not knowing how to find the open air,
But toiling desperately to find it out –
Torment myself to catch the English crown;
180 And from that torment I will free myself,
Or hew my way out with a bloody axe.
Why I can smile, and murder while I smile,
And cry 'Content!' to that which grieves my heart,
And wet my cheeks with artificial tears,
And frame my face to all occasions.
I'll drown more sailors than the mermaid shall;
I'll slay more gazers than the basilisk;
I'll play the orator as well as Nestor,
Deceive more slily than Ulysses could,

And, like a Sinon, take another Troy.   190
I can add colours to the chameleon,
Change shapes with Proteus for advantages,
And set the murderous Machiavel to school.
Can I do this, and cannot get a crown?
Tut, were it farther off, I'll pluck it down.

V.vi.61–93

RICHARD

What! Will the aspiring blood of Lancaster
Sink in the ground? I thought it would have mounted.
See how my sword weeps for the poor King's death!
O, may such purple tears be alway shed
From those that wish the downfall of our house!
If any spark of life be yet remaining,
Down, down to hell; and say I sent thee thither,
    (*He stabs him again*)
I that have neither pity, love, nor fear.
Indeed, 'tis true that Henry told me of;
For I have often heard my mother say   70
I came into the world with my legs forward.
Had I not reason, think ye, to make haste,
And seek their ruin that usurped our right?
The midwife wondered and the women cried
'O, Jesus bless us, he is born with teeth!'
And so I was, which plainly signified
That I should snarl and bite and play the dog.
Then, since the heavens have shaped my body so,
Let hell make crooked my mind to answer it.
I have no brother, I am like no brother;   80
And this word 'love', which greybeards call divine,
Be resident in men like one another
And not in me; I am myself alone.
Clarence, beware; thou keepest me from the light.
But I will sort a pitchy day for thee;
For I will buzz abroad such prophecies
That Edward shall be fearful of his life,
And then, to purge his fear, I'll be thy death.
King Henry and the Prince his son are gone;
Clarence, thy turn is next, and then the rest,   90

Counting myself but bad till I be best.
I'll throw thy body in another room
And triumph, Henry, in thy day of doom.

Further Reading

Primary sources are noted in full in the text, and are indexed.

Barton, A.: 'Shakespeare and the Limits of Language', in *Shakespeare Survey 24* (Cambridge, 1971)

Bevington, D.: *Shakespeare's Language of Gesture* (Harvard, 1984)

Blackburn, R. H.:*Biblical Drama under the Tudors* (The Hague, 1971)

Briggs, J.: *This Stage-Play World: English Literature and its Background, 1580–1625* (Oxford, 1983)

Burke, P.: *The Renaissance Sense of the Past* (London, 1969)

Campbell, L. B.: *Shakespeare's Histories* (London, 1947)

Coghill, N.: *Shakespeare's Professional Skills* (Cambridge, 1964)

Cohen, M.: *Sensible Words: Linguistic Practice in England 1640–1785* (Baltimore, 1977)

Dessen, A. C.: *Elizabethan Drama and the Viewer's Eye* (Cambridge 1977)

Fabini, T.: *Shakespeare and the Emblem* (Szeged, 1984)

Foakes, R. A.: *Illustrations of the English Stage, 1580–1642* (London, 1985)

Fraser, R.: *The Language of Adam* (New York, 1977)

Frey, D.: *The First Tetralogy: Shakespeare's Scrutiny of the Tudor Myth* (The Hague, 1976)

Grassi, E.: *Rhetoric as Philosophy* (Pittsburgh, 1980)

Gurr, A.: *Playgoing in Shakespeare's London* (Cambridge, 1987)

——: *The Shakespearean Stage, 1574–1642* (Cambridge 1970)

Hattaway, M.: *Elizabethan Popular Theatre* (London, 1982)

Haynes, J.: 'The Elizabethan Audience on Stage', in *The Theatrical Space: Themes in Drama 9* (Cambridge, 1987)

Heninger jr, S. K.: *Touches of Sweet Harmony: Pythagorean Cosmology and Renaissance Poetics* (San Marino, Calif., 1974)

Hodges, C. W.: *The Globe Restored* (London, 1968)

Homan, S.: *Shakespeare's Theater of Presence: Language, Spectacle and the Audience* (London, 1987)

Jones, T. B. and Nicol, B. de B.: *Neoclassical Dramatic Criticism 1560–1770* (Cambridge, 1976)

Joseph, B. L.: *Elizabethan Acting* (Oxford, 1951)

——: *Shakespeare's Eden* (London, 1971)

Kelly, H. A.: *Divine Providence and the England of Shakespeare's Histories* (Cambridge, Mass., 1970)

Knights, L. C.: *Shakespeare's Politics*, Annual Lecture of the British Academy (London, 1957)

Mahood, M. M.: *Shakespeare's Wordplay* (Oxford, 1967)

Mandrou, R.: *From Humanism to Science, 1480–1700* (Harmondsworth, 1978)

Moseley, C. W. R. D.: *Shakespeares's History Plays: 'Richard II' to 'Henry V': The Making of a King* (Harmondsworth 1988)

Ornstein, R.: *A Kingdom for a Stage* (Cambridge, Mass., 1972)

Padley, C. A.: *Grammatical Theory in Western Europe 1500–1700* (Cambridge, 1976)

Prior, M. E.: *The Dream of Power,* (Evanston, Illinois, 1973)

Reed, R. R.: *Crime and God's Judgement in Shakespeare* (London, 1985)

Ribner, I.: *The English History Play* (Princeton, 1965)

Righter, A.: *The Idea of the Play* (London, 1962)

Rose, M.: *Shakespearean Design* (Cambridge, Mass., 1972)

Rossiter, A. P.: *Angel with Horns* (London, 1961)

Saccio, P.: *Shakespeare's English Kings: History, Chronicle and Drama* (Oxford, 1977)

Schoenbaum, S. and Muir, K.: *A New Companion to Shakespeare Studies,* (Cambridge, 1971)

Smith, I.: *Shakespeare's Globe Playhouse: a Modern Reconstruction* (London, 1956)

Styan, J. L.: *Shakespeare's Stagecraft* (Cambridge, 1967)

Thomson, P.: *Shakespeare's Theatre* (London, 1983)

Tillyard, E. M. W.: *Shakespeare's English History Plays* (London, 1944)

——: *The Elizabethan World Picture* (London, 1943)

Toliver, H. E.: 'Falstaff, the Prince, and the History Play', in *Shakespeare Quarterly,* 16 (1965)

Traversi, D.: *Shakespeare from* Richard II *to* Henry V (London, 1957)

Vickers, B. (ed.): *The Artistry of Shakespeare's Prose* (Cambridge, 1968)

——: *Rhetoric revalued* (New York, 1982)

Wells, S.: *The Cambridge Companion to Shakespeare Studies* (Cambridge, 1987)

—— (ed.): *Shakespeare Survey 38* (Cambridge, 1985)

Wickham, G.: *Early English Stages, 1300–1660* (London, 1959–80)

——: *Shakespeare's Dramatic Heritage* (London, 1969)

Wikander, M. H.: *The Play of Truth and State: Historical Drama from Shakespeare to Brecht* (Baltimore, 1986)

Winny, J.: *The Player King* (Cambridge, 1968)

Wrightson, K.: *English Society 1580–1680* (London, 1982)

Yates, F.: *Astraea* (London, 1970)